AWAKENING
TO
MINDFULNESS

AWAKENING TO MINDFULNESS

10 Steps for Positive Change

Richard Fields, Ph.D.

Health Communications, Inc.
Deerfield Beach, Florida

www.hcibooks.com

Library of Congress Cataloging-in-Publication Data
is available through the Library of Congress.

ISBN-10: 0-7573-0668-3
ISBN-13: 978-0-7573-0668-6

Publisher: Health Communications, Inc.
3201 S.W. 15th Street
Deerfield Beach, FL 33442-8190

Cover design by Jesse Colter
Interior design and formatting by Dawn Von Strolley Grove

To my brother Barry,
whose spirit lives on
in my son Matthew
and within me as well.

CONTENTS

ACKNOWLEDGMENTS

A special thanks to my friends and colleagues who helped review the manuscript and made valuable suggestions for the book: Alan Berger, Ph.D.; Tara Brach, Ph.D.; Michael Leeds, Ph.D.; Alan Marlatt, Ph.D.; Ronald Siegal, Psy.D.; Nancy Sobel, Ph.D.; and Michael Yapko, Ph.D. Thank you also to the staff at HCI Books.

PREFACE

Awakening to Mindfulness: 10 Steps for Positive Change is the first in a series of Minestrone for the Mind books. This book focuses on ten steps that promote healthy, positive change and mindful living. Much like a bowl of minestrone soup, it is a specific collection of ideas and insights that are the ingredients for a more mindful life. Future books in the series will build on this one to help you further understand mindfulness.

Minestrone Soup

Minestrone soup is a mixture of ingredients that, with the proper balance, creates a soothing, tender, and enriching full-bodied taste. The key to good minestrone is the freshness and the proper mix of ingredients and the right spicing. This also metaphorically describes mindfulness:

Freshness—Being in the present ("in the now"), the freshness of what life's ingredients are today.

Mix of ingredients—A balance, an awareness, concentrating on the variety in life and the changing mixes of experiences each day.

Spicing—The right focus and concentration, to include compassionate communication, wonder, and courage each day.

Cooking Minestrone

Awakening to Mindfulness, the first in the Minestrone for the Mind series, has been simmering for many years. Good books don't just happen. They are a result of years of experience, the three *p*'s (passion, perseverance, and patience), hard work, support, and the most important element, timely application.

This book draws upon my experience as a conference developer. For the past fifteen years I have developed and produced approximately one hundred mental health and alcohol/drug recovery conferences under the auspices of my company, FACES Conferences (Family and Addiction Conferences and Educational Services). We have trained thousands of mental health and alcohol/drug counselors.

I have invited speakers who are leaders in their fields to present at these conferences. Minestrone for the Mind draws upon the expertise of these talented, dynamic, and creative "master" teachers. The ten mindful steps include information gleaned from these presenters.

This book is also influenced by my more than thirty years in the counseling field. I have specialized in the noble and difficult journey of helping individuals and families recover from alcohol and drug dependence and addiction. I have found tremendous benefit in using mindfulness practices in helping clients overcome alcohol/drug problems and as a tool for relapse prevention. My counseling work has strongly influenced this book, and you will find many applications throughout the book that stem from my experience in the addictions field.

Master Publishing Chefs

The essential ingredient in creating Minestrone for the Mind came from two accomplished publishing chefs: Gary Seidler and Peter Vegso, owners of Health Communications, Inc., and the original publishers of the very popular Chicken Soup for the Soul series. They liked the concepts in the original *Awakening to Mindfulness* manuscript and helped guide the book throughout the process.

Awakening to Mindfulness

There has been a rise in both the interest in and information on mindfulness in the last ten years in the United States. However, mindfulness is a concept that is often difficult to assimilate in Western culture. The Buddhist concepts of letting go, embracing emptiness and separateness, meditation practices, body awareness, not controlling, and giving up of ego are difficult concepts and practices for us to understand and even more difficult to integrate and assimilate into our everyday lives. This book is an introduction to mindfulness. It is an invitation to help you develop awareness of and interest in (awakening to) mindfulness practices in your own life.

Mindfulness: A Powerful Tool for Healing

Mindfulness is a powerful healing tool that promotes personal growth, mental health, and emotional, physical, and spiritual well-being.

The counseling field has been exploring the application of mindfulness for a number of years now in the treatment of a variety of disorders. Meditation, mindfulness practices, and Buddhist teachings (dharma) have proven to be beneficial in addressing many physical and psychological problems, from back pain to sleep disorders, depression, anxiety, and so on.

John Kabat-Zinn used mindfulness-based stress reduction to help patients with pain, as well as patients with anxiety disorders (Kabat-Zinn 1992). Marsha Linehan (1993) integrated mindfulness practices in her dialectical behavior therapy (DBT) for the treatment of borderline personality disorders. Steven Hayes (1999) developed a mindfulness model called acceptance and commitment therapy (ACT). Mindfulness-based cognitive therapy (MBCT) was developed by Zindel Segal and associates (2002) as a relapse prevention approach to depression.

Many clinicians in the alcohol/drug recovery and mental health fields (including myself) are using meditation and mindfulness practices as an effective, positive, and beneficial part of their counseling practices.

Alan Marlatt, Ph.D., cites Groves and Farmer (1994) as defining addiction through the Buddhist perspective, as a "false refuge." Marlatt notes: "As I continued my reading I became more aware that the Buddhist literature offers considerable insight into the basic nature of addiction, how addictive behavior develops, and how meditation can be used as a method of transcending a wide variety of addictive problems." (2002)

Marlatt has been developing a mindfulness-based relapse prevention (MBRP) approach to help individuals in alcohol/drug recovery to deal more effectively with cravings and urges, and to prevent alcohol/drug lapses and relapses.

Mindfulness has also been used effectively to help people age better and to live healthier and longer lives. In

1976, Ellen Langer and Judith Rodin conducted a study with elderly nursing-home residents. The experimental group was encouraged to be actively involved in decision making (everything from choosing activities to caring for a plant). The results were startling. Eighteen months after the experiment, 30 percent (thirteen of forty-four) of the control group had died, compared to 15 percent (seven of forty-seven) in the experimental group.

Mindfulness is emerging as a "healing" tool for more and more human conditions. Whether it is living longer, healthier, and more engaged lives, or learning new skills and overcoming problematic behaviors (for example, alcoholism/drug addiction), mindfulness is a beneficial healing too, that can be used in some way by everyone. Mindfulness helps heal wounds, allows for forgiveness, and helps us have more compassion for ourselves and others. Mindfulness is a healing tool for our own spirits, the spirit of our families, our communities, our country, other nations, and our world.

Buddhism—"A Living Psychology"

Buddhist teacher and psychologist Jack Kornfield, Ph.D., a leader in the mindfulness field, describes Buddhism as a form of psychology. He describes Buddha's teachings as a "living psychology" with a focus on helping individuals to find their "freedom." He writes in *The Wise Heart*: "Buddhist masters . . . are practitioners of a living psychology: one of the oldest and most well-developed systems of healing and understanding on the face of the earth." In a 2007 interview in *Inquiring Mind*, Kornfield points out the extreme differences in approach between the clinical psychology field and the "psychology of Buddhism":

Clinical Psychology	**Psychology of Buddhism**
Focus on pathology	Focus on living and freedom
25 states of depression	25 states of rapture
A list of anxiety disorders	A list of states of extreme trust and contentment
Emphasis on independence	Emphasis on interdependence

Benefits of Incorporating Mindfulness Practices in Your Life

This is a book of "attraction" to mindfulness. The goal of this book is to awaken you to the benefits of incorporating mindfulness practices in your own life. The benefits of mindfulness are profound, yet often misunderstood. *Awakening to Mindfulness* demystifies mindfulness and gives you straightforward and pragmatic ways to apply mindfulness in your life. You don't have to be a Zen master or become a Buddhist or make dramatic changes in your life to experience the benefits of mindfulness.

By reading this book and doing the exercises and meditation at the end of each mindful step, you can better explore your own understanding of mindfulness. Hopefully, you will experience some of the benefits of incorporating mindfulness practices into your own life. Establishing mindfulness "rituals" will help you stabilize and balance your life, even in the most tumultuous of times, and enhance your well-being in a deep, profound, and meaningful way.

A basic understanding of some of the laws and principles of mindfulness (dharma) can help you to:

- Better understand and improve your relationships with friends, family, and others
- Improve your relationship with your spouse/partner
- Improve your parenting, giving new energy to your relationships with your children (at both younger and older ages)
- Find a more effective way of interacting in your work life that enhances your relationships with colleagues and promotes success
- Deal with stress, time, and life management
- Be more balanced

- Appreciate life more, having gratitude
- Have the ability to stay "in the now"

Additional benefits include:

- Stress reduction
- Being able to overcome anger and reactivity and being more reflective
- The ability to relax and overcome obsessive ruminative thinking
- Relief from anxiety and depression
- The ability to better deal with conflict and rejection
- The ability to accept oneself and others
- Being able to make connections with others, nature, and self

A major benefit of mindfulness is that you will have more appreciation and recognition for the "joy" in your life.

I invite and encourage you to come on this journey!

Section One: Foundation

Introduction: UNDERSTANDING AND DEFINING MINDFULNESS

"Listen with the third ear, and
let the dharma rain fall."

—The Buddha

The term "mindfulness" is now being used quite liberally to mean a variety of things. There are different dimensions and levels of mindfulness, from basic "awareness" to deeper and more meaningful senses of enlightenment. Mindfulness has different dimensions and impacts both the body and mind. This introduction will give you definitions and content to help clarify what I mean by mindfulness. Various quotes from leaders in the mindfulness field are included to help you better grasp its essence.

The Eightfold Path

The Eightfold Path is the foundation of Buddhist teachings. A brief summary of the path and the Four Noble Truths will help you better understand the underpinnings of mindfulness. Mindfulness is the seventh stage of the Eightfold Path. The eight stages are:

1. Right view
2. Right intention
3. Right speech
4. Right action
5. Right livelihood
6. Right effort
7. Right mindfulness
8. Right concentration

The term "right" in the Eightfold Path is used not in the context of "right" or "wrong," but instead as the preferred way or suggested way. "Right" also means wholeheartedness and goodness.

The Eightfold Path has also been described as an eight-step training in "fire management." Fire is the ego. The Eightfold Path is a kind of shelter for the fire of the ego.

1. Right View

Right view involves not only seeing but also grasping the "impermanence" and "imperfection" of all things, ideas, and life in general. Right view sees things as they are with an open and accommodating attitude. There is joy in this simple, straightforward approach to life "in the now," moment to moment. Right view is described as a concept of wisdom, and it resides in all aspects of the mind, not just the intellect.

Right view also involves an openness to listen and consider what is right and wrong dispassionately. Opinionatedness is when one invests his or her ego in a view.

"You have to be alert when you are playing
with fire. To make a useful fire, we begin
by creating a sheltered fireplace, and
bringing together fuel and a spark.
All of these initial steps fall with the Right View. Our inner life
must be sheltered from the ego wind."

—David Brazier, *The Feeling Buddha*

"It is attachment to opinions that leads
to the fire of our passion getting out of control."
—David Brazier, *The Feeling Buddha*

Right view is further defined by the Four Noble Truths.

THE FOUR NOBLE TRUTHS

- ***First Noble Truth: Life means suffering.*** Right view involves the intuitive insight that all beings, human and animal alike, are subject to suffering. Our American culture does a good job of trying to avoid, ignore, distract from, not see, and deny "suffering." But suffering is a natural part of life and death. During our lifetime, each of us will endure all kinds of suffering:

  Physical suffering—pain, illness, injury, fatigue, disease, old age, and death.

  Psychological suffering—anxiety, loneliness, boredom, frustration, trauma, depression, and so on.

Interpersonal suffering—loss, betrayal, injustice, violation, heartbreak, and more.

Unfortunately, our Western culture avoids this first noble truth, and we are therefore surprised when the distractions do not work and our own denial and delusion are shattered.

- ***Second Noble Truth: The origin of suffering is attachments.*** This second noble truth describes attachment as craving and clinging. This arises in desire, passion, drive for wealth and prestige, striving for fame and popularity, and so on. Attachment includes living life through our children, spouse, or job. Letting go of attachments involves giving up our expectations about how we think things should be. This truth is also hard to accept in our Western culture. There is the illusion that if we are wealthy we will be safe from suffering and harm.

- ***Third Noble Truth: The cessation of suffering is attainable.*** This third noble truth has as its focus that "dispassion" can end suffering. Removing that "dispassion" can end suffering. By removing the cause of suffering (attachment in the form of craving and clinging), one can develop dispassion, which can lead to a state of Nirvana. "Nirvana" is defined as freedom from all worries, troubles, and self-fabricated concerns and ideas.

- ***Fourth Noble Truth: The path to the cessation of suffering is the "middle way."*** This fourth noble truth describes a cessation of suffering by a gradual path of self-improvement. This is described as a balanced middle way between the excessive attachment of craving and clinging and the ascetic way of self-denial and self-mortification. Metaphorically, this is described as the middle of the river where the current is strongest. For example, in deciding to lose weight, the middle way would neither be a compulsive, controlling, craving to lose as much weight as possible in an imbalanced perception of thinness (an eating disorder), nor an ascetic approach of not eating or eating very little. Instead, the middle way would involve a gradual balance in being more mindfully aware of how we eat, what we eat, and what quantities we eat, balanced with proper nutrition and exercise.

The result would be more enjoyment of food, better nutrition, a healthier body, a more mindful awareness of the body, and an integration of body and mind.

2. Right Intention

Intention is that mental energy that controls our actions. It involves volition (willpower) to commit to ethical and virtuous intentions, which lead to goodness in actions and self-improvement.

Buddha described three types of right intentions as follows:

1. The intention of renunciation, which means the resistance to the pull of desire
2. The intention of good will, which means resistance to feelings of anger and aversion
3. The intention of harmlessness, which means not to think or act cruelly, violently, or aggressively and to develop compassion

Right intention is sometimes described as having right thought and using and developing all our intentions, thoughts, and skills to cultivate peace.

Right intention or right thought describes fifteen defilements or seeds of further suffering. The fifteen defilements are intentions/thoughts of:

1. Greed
2. Ill will

3. Hostility
4. Denigration
5. Dominance
6. Envy
7. Jealousy
8. Hypocrisy
9. Fraud
10. Obstinacy
11. Presumption
12. Conceit
13. Arrogance
14. Vanity
15. Negligence

3. Right Speech

Right speech is the first principle of ethical conduct in the Eightfold Path. Speech is powerful. Words can help create peace or wars, invoke compassion or hatred, heal or shame, join or divide, love or destroy. Right speech involves words of honesty, kindness, and nurturance. Right speech involves speaking only what is worthy and valuable for the moment. Buddha's guidelines for right speech involve telling the truth, speaking gently with warmth and friendliness, and talking only when necessary.

Right speech involves a voice of truthfulness, compassion, and helpfulness. For a more complete description of right speech, see Mindful Step #1: Invoke Compassion.

4. Right Action

The underlying principle of right action is that wholesome acts lead to sound states of mind, while unwholesome acts lead to unsound states. Right action means to abstain from:

- Harming others
- Taking what is not given—theft, robbery, fraud, deceitfulness, and dishonesty
- Sexual misconduct

Right actions do good for others, for the good of the world. Being the best that we can be is right action.

5. Right Livelihood

Right livelihood is when one earns a living in a righteous and good way—in a way that makes a contribution to society, doing good work that benefits others. Money and wealth should be gained legally, ethically, and peacefully. Right livelihood should also be performed properly, with attention to detail. Any occupations that violate the principles of right speech and right action should be avoided.

6. Right Effort

"Right effort is the activity of
tending the fire once it is underway."
—David Brazier, *The Feeling Buddha*

"Mental energy" is the force behind right effort. Wrong effort is struggle and aggression and is misguided when it distracts the mind from its task and causes confusion. Right effort is wholesome.

Wholesome Efforts	**Unwholesome Efforts**
Self-disciplined	Craving
Honest	Dishonest
Benevolent	Envious
Kind and gentle	Mean and aggressive
Compassionate	Uncaring

7. Right Mindfulness

A definition of mindfulness that is widely accepted is given by John Kabat-Zinn (1992):

> "The awareness that merges through paying attention on purpose, in the present moment, and nonjudgmentally to the unfolding of experience, moment by moment."

Right mindfulness is described later in this chapter in more detail.

8. Right Concentration

Right concentration is a single-minded concentration on the path to peace (the Eightfold Path). It is wholesome concentration in which we are completely absorbed "in the now," totally present and aware. The result of right concentration is the development of a mental force that is present in everyday life, a natural consciousness. The practice of meditation is integral in the development of right concentration. The practice of meditation helps to intensify concentration step by step so that concentration can be applied to everyday situations.

Mindfulness Versus Mindlessness

One way to help define mindfulness is to first describe "mindlessness." In her book *Mindfulness,* Ellen Langer, Ph.D., a Harvard professor, researcher, and author, has several early chapters that ironically focus on "mindlessness." She describes this habitual and automatic mindlessness as a lack of orientation, concentration, focus, and awareness of what is going on "in the now" (the present). She illustrates mindlessness with this comical story:

> Once in a mall department store, I gave a cashier a new credit card. Noticing that I hadn't signed it, she handed it back to me to sign. Then she took my card, passed it through her machine, handed me the resulting form and asked me to sign it. I did as I was told. The cashier then held the form next to the newly signed card to see if the signature matched.

In defining mindfulness, Langer reminds us to be aware of the costs of "mindlessness" and the benefits of "mindfulness."

Definitions of Mindfulness

"Mindfulness" can be defined many ways. It can be defined as attention, awareness, and remembering (remembering to pay attention). Mindfulness is also about remembering to experience (not escape from) all aspects of life, including the pain and sorrow and the simple things we do as well as the magnificent things in life.

"We could say that the word mindfulness
is pointing to being one with our experience,
not dissociating, being right there
when our hand touches the doorknob
or the telephone rings or feelings
of all kinds arise."

—Pema Chodron, *When Things Fall Apart*

Enjoying the simple acts of walking, talking, listening, or any of our bodily senses (the smell and taste of food, the touch of a loved one) are all acts of mindfulness if we remember to enjoy and be present with them.

"Take my hand and we will walk together.
We will look at flowers and smile
at passers-by. Our walking will be like
a beautiful song, a melody that flows on
without haste. The point is not
to get somewhere. The point is
to enjoy something lovely and satisfying.
If we do so then we are fulfilling
the higher purpose."

—David Brazier, *The Feeling Buddha*

Mindfulness: Experiencing the Pleasant and Unpleasant

"Mindfulness has to do with
the quality of both awareness and participation
that a person brings to everyday life."

—Steven Hayes, Victoria Follette, and
Marsha Linehan, *Mindfulness and Acceptance*

Mindfulness involves being present to experience the wonders of life, as well as the hardships. Mindfulness involves both the joy of the birth of a child as well as the sorrow of the death of a loved one. It is the ability to embrace life and living while having compassion for our own and others' suffering. It is being fully present.

"Awakening is found in our pleasure
and our pain, our confusion and our wisdom,
available in each moment of our weird,
unfathomable, ordinary everyday lives."

—Pema Chodron, *When Things Fall Apart*

Instead of avoiding unpleasant feelings, you can learn to look at these feelings with awe, even surprise—not judging, but instead putting them at arm's length. You may even laugh at your vulnerability and how easily and quickly you can lose your way.

You can learn to embrace the fragile changing nature and cycles of your own life. Mindfulness is nonjudgmental, a taking in of what is, embracing the change moment to moment.

"Broadly conceptualized mindfulness
has been described as a nonelaborative,
nonjudgmental, present-centered awareness
in which each thought, feeling, or sensation
that arises in the attentional field is
acknowledged and accepted as it is. . . ."

—Mark Lau and Zindel Segal,
"Mindfulness-Based Cognitive Therapy
as a Relapse Prevention Approach to Depression"

Later in this chapter, I will show you how to best utilize this book and suggest a program and resources that can help guide you to a better understanding of mindfulness and the discovery of your Buddha nature. In her book *Radical Acceptance*, psychologist and Buddhist meditation teacher Tara Brach defines "Buddha nature" as "recognizing our essential goodness, our natural wisdom and compassion."

Mindfulness: A Condition of Compassion and Heart for Peace, Tranquility, and Goodness

"Even the most exalted states and the most
exceptional spiritual accomplishmensts are unimportant
if we cannot be happy in the most basic and ordinary ways,
if we cannot touch one another and the life
we have been given with our hearts."

—Jack Kornfield, *A Path with Heart*

The word "mind" has an association with the brain or the head. You might think of "mindfulness" as residing in your head. Yet "heart" is the pivotal and essential element of mindfulness.

A good minestrone soup, or for that matter any creation, requires a heartfelt involvement. The same holds true for mindfulness. In speaking of mindfulness, Jack Kornfield (*A Path with Heart*) reminds us that the mindful path must include heart: "We must make certain that our path is connected with our heart."

Having compassion for our own suffering and the suffering of others, we can apply mindfulness principles with a fullness and richness that benefits everyone. Mindfulness practice with heart creates a sense of well-being that is contagious. The energy created by our compassion leads to a community and world that is one of peace, tranquility, and goodness.

How to Effectively Use This Book

First Step: Quiet Western Cynicism

In order to allow yourself to experience the full impact and benefit of this book, you need to put your analytical, cognitive-solution-focused Western thinking aside. Being critical of the precepts and teachings of this book will distract you from the essence of mindfulness. When you find yourself doubting and critically saying to yourself, "That won't work," or "That doesn't make sense," try to wait, putting those thoughts at arm's length. Do not judge; instead, be present. Be gentle with yourself and let go, trying to assimilate to and accommodate mindfulness. I strongly suggest that you invoke the mantra given for each mindful step, complete the learning activities, and practice the meditations to gain a fuller and richer experience of mindfulness. I also encourage you to read more about mindfulness and Buddhism and attend a mindfulness retreat and dharma lectures as a follow-up to this book.

Read Each Mindful Step with Gentle Concentration

I suggest you take your time reading each chapter. Read each mindful step slowly, allowing your mind to reflect on the content and message. I also suggest that you reread each step as often as you like to keep each one in consciousness. I have found it extremely beneficial to read a step out loud to a loved one as a bedtime ritual.

Start Journaling

After reading a mindful step chapter, journal your thoughts, feelings, even physical sensations. Note what comes up and write about it in your journal, without judging what comes into your consciousness. Especially note any resistance and any insights.

EACH MINDFUL STEP HAS A MANTRA

A "mantra" is a word that you can repeat over and over to yourself. For example, the first mindful step has to do with invoking compassion and being less critical of others. The mantra for this step is "compassion." You repeat the mantra "compassion" to yourself silently over and over, to remind yourself to focus on being compassionate. When you are losing your way, you might invoke the mantra "compassion," reminding yourself to be less critical of others, while invoking compassion for yourself and others.

The following chart shows the mantra for each mindful step:

Mindful Step	Mantra
#1 Invoke Compassion	*Compassion*
#2 Stop Being So Hard on Yourself	*Acceptance*
#3 Maintain a Good Attitude	*Attitude*
#4 Opening Up to "Discovery"	*Discovery*

Mindful Step		Mantra
#5	Embrace Positive and Healthy Change	*Change*
#6	Stay "in the Now"	*Now*
#7	Recognize Vulnerable States of Body and Mind	*HALTS*
#8	Embrace Healthy Habits—Exercise and Flow	*Flow*
#9	Make Connections	*Connection*
#10	Focus on the Ten Elements of Success	*Success*

Make Each Mindful Step the Focus

To help keep each mindful step in consciousness, you can make one mindful step and its accompanying mantra the focus for the week. I encourage you to repeat the mantra to yourself for twenty minutes in the morning and twenty minutes in the late afternoon each day for one week. You can reread the chapter to regain the essence of the step. You can doodle or write the mantra for the step when you are on the phone or sitting in a meeting. I encourage you to do this for each mindful step.

Complete the Mindful Activities

Each mindful step also features suggested activities that help reinforce that step. These activities will greatly enhance your understanding and application of each mindful step. If you have difficulty completing the mindful activities, you might ask someone close to you to help you complete them.

Practice the Meditations

Each mindful step includes a meditation, an extremely valuable tool that can help you slow down, relax, and focus on being more centered, in the "middle way." The meditations are designed as a practice of "Right Concentration" and a way to focus and reinforce the "mantra/message" of that mindful step. Read the meditation as the culminating experience for each mindful step.

Journal Again

After reading each chapter, you've been asked to journal, focus on the mantra, reread the mindful step, complete the mindful activities, and do the meditation. Once you've done that, it is time to go back to your journal and write whatever comes to mind. It will be interesting to reread your first entry in the journal for that mindful step to see if there is an expanded awareness or any changes in your focus.

This Is *Your* Journey!

I invite and encourage you to come on this journey. Please remember this is *your* journey. There is no one way or right way to come to understand and develop mindfulness. Each individual follows his or her own path, and there are many different paths. Please find the path that works best for you.

"It has been customary to speak of
the spiritual path as if it were something
like a well-marked highway with
entrance ramps and speed limits
and even rest stops or service stations.
People speak of being 'on the path'
as if it were clear where it starts and stops."

—Mark Epstein, *Going to Pieces Without Falling Apart*

Mindful Step #1:
INVOKE COMPASSION

Goal: I will be less critical of myself and others and more compassionate.

Mantra: COMPASSION

DOING NO HARM

Do not take lightly small misdeeds,
Believing they can do no harm.
Even a tiny spark of fire
Can set alight a mountain of hay.

ACTING FOR THE GOOD

Do not take lightly small good deeds,
Believing they can hardly help.
For drops of water one by one
In time can fill a giant pot.

—Patrul Rinpoch,
The Words of My Perfect Teacher

Compassion for Self and Others

"Relative bodhicitta (a term used in the
Tibetan traditions) is the practice of
compassion and compassionate action.
Compassion is the strong and deep feeling
that wants to alleviate the suffering of beings,
and it arises when we allow ourselves
to come close to suffering both
our own and that of others."

—Joseph Goldstein, *One Dharma*

Compassion is the practice of recognizing and being sensitive to others' suffering as well as to one's own. To be compassionate means to be present with others' pain and suffering. Compassion is a heartfelt emotion that includes understanding, sensitivity, tolerance, support, and care. It is hard to be compassionate toward others when you are emotionally blocked by your own fears. In order to be more compassionate toward others, you need to heal your own suffering. You need a "tender heart" to be available to others. Compassion also involves "loving-kindness practices." These are practices of caring and loving others, showing them kindness and concern.

Resisting the Temptation to Be Critical of Others

Compassion involves being gentle instead of reactive (or harsh), being affirming instead of critical, and being present in painful times instead of withdrawing and putting up walls.

It is good to be:

- Less critical and more courteous
- Consciously aware of helping others
- Seeing and respecting others
- Aware of our mutual interaction and mutual consciousness

This might be as simple as holding the door open for someone rather than letting it go because you are in a hurry. You need to acknowledge others, especially those who are less fortunate than you.

Being Reflective Instead of Reactive

A negative, reactive attitude toward others causes harm. Being respectful, gentle, and reflective is a better way to be.

"We become so expert at causing harm
to ourselves and others. The trick then
is to practice gentleness and letting go."

—Pema Chodron, *When Things Fall Apart*

The Buddhist expression "Don't talk about injured limbs" means don't talk negatively about others' defects.

"Paying attention to another's faults
is just a distraction from paying attention
to what is happening right here and now."

—Ellen Birx, *Healing Zen*

"Don't draw another's bow;
Don't ride another's horse;
Don't speak of another's faults;
Don't try to know another's affairs."

—Zen Verse

Instead of focusing on the faults of others, it is best to focus on your own issues and challenges. Mindfulness involves recognizing your own faults, putting them at arm's length, smiling at how easily and quickly they can arise, and not letting them take over.

We need to recognize how our own denial and self-delusion can distract us from the path of mindfulness. It starts by recognizing how "the fire of our ego" will blind us to our self-deception.

Many times while I am counseling others, we sit and smile together as we recognize how we trick ourselves. We smile at the self-deception, recognizing how easily it can be invoked.

> "Because of mindfulness, we see our desires
> and our aggression, our jealousy and
> our ignorance. We don't act on them;
> we just see them. Without mindfulness,
> we don't see them and they proliferate."
>
> —Pema Chodron, *Comfortable with Uncertainty*

Critical Attitudes

"The thought manifests as the word;
The word manifests as the deed;
The deed develops into habit;
And habit hardens into character.

So watch the thought and its ways with care,
And let it spring from love,

Born out of concern for all beings."

—The Buddha (in Sharon Salzberg, *Lovingkindness*)

Greed, Hatred, and Delusion

Three critical attitudes that create problems are *greed, hatred,* and *delusion*.

Being self-focused and greedy is an aggressive attitude that does not consider the needs of others nor the long-term impact of our actions on the community. This greediness can include being discourteous, disregarding others' feelings, dishonesty, and acting on resentments, as well as polluting the environment and waging war.

Hatred is another attitude that harms others. This includes discrimination, prejudice, bigotry, and revenge.

Delusion is a way to justify actions that are harmful to others and self. Instead of invoking these harmful attitudes and actions, you can focus on *generosity, love,* and *awareness* (see below).

CHANGING CRITICAL ATTITUDES

GREED to GENEROSITY

HATRED to LOVE

DELUSION to AWARENESS

Blame: A Form of Criticism and Avoidance of Responsibility

Blame is just another form of criticism and a way to avoid looking at your own responsibility.

"Blaming is a way to protect our hearts to try to protect what is soft and open and tender in ourselves. Rather than own the pain, we scramble to find some comfortable ground."

— Pema Chodron, *When Things Fall Apart*

"You made me . . ." statements, such as "You made me angry," or "You made me do this," are ways of not taking responsibility for our own feelings. Blaming and holding on to blame keeps us stuck, isolated, and alone—like "a dragon in the corner eating our own tail."

"We habitually erect a barrier called blame
that keeps us from communicating
genuinely with others, and we fortify
it with our concepts of who's right
and who's wrong. . . ."

—Pema Chodron, *When Things Fall Apart*

Complaining

There is a difference between giving feedback and complaining. Feedback, done properly, is respectful to others and communicates ways to address a problem. Complaining and putting someone down is not necessary and does not help a situation.

People often complain about things that are not in their control. Recently I was flying from the East Coast to the West Coast. I overheard a man complaining about the long flight ahead of him. When the announcement was made that the flight was delayed due to thunderstorms, the man blew up, complaining loudly, so everyone could hear his dissatisfaction.

Despite the airline staff's explanation that safety was the priority, he continued to complain. He complained about the airline, the weather in this region this time of year, and so on. Complaining about things that are out of our control is a way to feel sorry for ourselves. It is not respectful, nor is it helpful in accepting or resolving the situation.

"See if you can catch yourself
complaining, in either speech or thought,
about a situation you find yourself in,
what other people do or say, your surroundings,
your life situation, even the weather."

—Eckhart Tolle, *The Power of Now*

Practicing Right Speech

As mentioned in the Introduction, "right speech" is an essential component of the Buddhist Eightfold Path. Speech is very powerful. Your words, your delivery, and your emphasis can cause a wide range of reactions, from great harm to significant good.

Instead of being critical, judgmental, and aggressive, your speech can be affirming, understanding, and gentle.

> "Unskillful words can start wars or feuds
> and lead those who are close to us
> to suffer deeply. Skillful speech
> can open hearts, lead to deep insights,
> and promote healing and transformation."
>
> —Donald Rothberg, *The Engaged Spiritual Life*

Right Speech is described by Buddha as having:

- Truthfulness
- Helpfulness
- Kindness
- Goodwill
- Appropriateness

It is spoken at the right time. It is spoken in truth. It is spoken affectionately. It is spoken beneficially. It is spoken with a mind of goodwill.

Right speech involves truthfulness and giving up all forms of false speech, as well as gray areas of truthfulness such as exaggerations, half-truths, omissions, and denials.

Right speech involves giving up malicious speech; abstaining from harsh speech, gossip, and rumors; and embracing good, gentle, and caring speech.

> "Giving up harsh speech and abstaining
> from harsh speech, one speaks words
> that are gentle, pleasing to the ear,
> and lovable, that reach the heart,
> that are courteous and agreeable to others."
>
> —Donald Rothberg, *The Engaged Spiritual Life*

The ultimate goal of right speech is to help establish safety in relationships, which leads to trust—a trust that promotes peace, cooperation, and well-being among people in our communities and our world.

Cherishing Instead of Criticizing

Couples need to be mindful of "cherishing" their partners, not disparaging them. We need to care about them, treating them well and with respect. Be more affirming, approving, open, truthful, and involved in close relationships.

Putting your "heart" into close relationships means having integrity and honesty.

"Many of us begin a relationship
with great love, very intense love.
So intense that we believe that,
without our partner, we cannot survive.
Yet if we do not practice mindfulness,
it takes only one or two years
for our love to be transformed into hatred.
Then, in our partner's presence
we have the opposite feeling; we feel terrible.
It becomes impossible to live together anymore,
so divorce is the only way.
Love has been transformed into hatred;
our flower has become garbage."

—Thich Nhat Hanh, *Taming the Tiger Within*

In his book *Why Marriages Succeed or Fail*, John Gottman, a noted authority on marital relationships, illustrates the dramatic impact of critical/judgmental communication between couples. In his couples lab at the University of Washington, Gottman was able to quantitatively document four key factors that predict divorce. Gottman labeled them the "four horsemen of the apocalypse of relationships." They are *criticism, contempt, defensiveness,* and *stonewalling.*

Criticism is toxic to partner/marital relationships. Couples who have a higher ratio of critical comments toward each other, compared to affirming comments, have a much higher probability of divorce or a break up.

Contempt between couples is demonstrated nonverbally with rolled eyes, a ticking sound of the tongue, a smirk, a sarcastic laugh, turning of the head, and so on. These nonverbal behaviors essentially give the message to the spouse that he or she is "dumb" or "stupid."

Defensiveness is usually in the form of "tireless debates" in which couples do not take ownership for what they say and do. Couples will argue about details and who said what to distract from the issues. They will also distract by bringing up unrelated, unresolved conflicts from the past (a "litany of backlogged resentments"). Defensive couples will not listen to each other, nor seek to understand. In their defensiveness they avoid taking responsibility for their own inappropriate statements and behaviors. They defend against taking responsibility for their critical behavior and fail to apologize or make amends.

Stonewalling, or withdrawal, can take many forms, but

the purpose is the same: I am going to punish you by shutting down. This is a very childish defense mechanism, much like pouting or taking your ball and leaving the game when things don't go your way.

You can see how criticism, contempt, defensiveness, and stonewalling are all behaviors that block communication and make intimacy difficult to attain in partner/marital relationships. Listening and being affirming and compassionate are the essential "mindful" qualities that need to be embraced rather than criticism, contempt, defensiveness, and stonewalling.

"The major obstacle of love, I have found,
is a premature walling off of
the personality that results in
a falseness or inauthenticity
that other people can feel.
Love, after all, requires a person
to be open and vulnerable,
able to tolerate and enjoy the crossing
of ego boundaries that occurs
naturally under the spell of passion."
—Mark Epstein, *Going to Pieces Without Falling Apart*

COMPASSION

Having compassion and being less critical of others means:

- Being sensitive to others' suffering as well as your own
- Being reflective (gentle) instead of reactive
- Changing critical attitudes (greed, hatred, delusion) into generosity, love, awareness
- Being truthful, helpful, kind, and appropriate
- Not blaming (taking responsibility)
- Not complaining
- Invoking right speech
- "Cherishing" others
- Avoiding and reducing criticism, contempt, defensiveness, and stonewalling in partner relationships
- Having the grace to love and be loved

Mindful Activities for Invoking Compassion

Your Mantra Is "Compassion"

Remember that your mantra is "compassion." Invoke your mantra to remind yourself to be compassionate toward others and yourself. You can start your day by repeating your mantra "compassion" in morning meditation. When conflict arises, invoke compassion. Think of others and be available and present "in the now" to help others. Invoke "right speech," "right thoughts," and "right action," all of which are done with compassion.

Reread This Step to Yourself

Reread this step to yourself. This will keep compassion as the focus and remind you to invoke compassion and right speech in your daily life. Because compassion is so integral to mindfulness, I suggest that you reread this step periodically to refocus on compassion.

Read This Step Out Loud to Someone Close to You

It would be beneficial to read this entire step out loud to

someone close to you and to talk with him or her about it. It can become a nice ritual for partners to read a mindful step out loud to each other before going to sleep.

Make a List of People You Care About

In your journal, list all of the people you care about. Then give each person on your list a phone call, write a letter, or send an e-mail. Tell them you care about them and are just letting them know you are thinking about them.

Write an Unsolicited Letter of Appreciation to Someone Who Has Shown You Compassion

Write a letter to someone who has had a positive influence on your life and has shown you compassion. Thank this person for his or her compassion and share the impact he or she had on you. Don't tell the person you are sending the letter; let it be a surprise.

After you have completed the above exercises, do something good for yourself (get a massage, take a long walk, or sit in nature).

Compassion Meditation

Find a comfortable place to sit. Make yourself comfortable, on a chair or couch with your back straight and your arms resting on your lap, palms up, holding your left hand in your right palm, with thumbs slightly touching.

Gently close your eyes and focus on your breath.

Breathe in slowly through your nose and exhale all your breath. Breathe in, filling your abdomen with air. Hold your breath counting to four, then exhale fully. Then breathe slowly and calmly for a few minutes.

Feel your body relax; your head is lighter; your neck has no tension. You might even want to stretch your neck from side to side, still breathing slowly.

You can relax your chest with a few deep breaths.

You can relax your belly, feeling the air fill it as you breathe in.

You can relax your hips, your butt, your legs. Feel the tension release from your legs.

You can flex and twist your feet as they relax as well.

Now slowly open your eyes and read the meditation to yourself.

Think of people close to you who might be going through a difficult time and/or experiencing emotional or physical pain and suffering.

Envision yourself coming to them and comforting them, having compassion for them, soothing their pain, hugging them, and telling them you are there for them.

Envision yourself as a child; comfort yourself as a child. Take your time as you hold yourself as a child.

Envision yourself as an adolescent; comfort and soothe the pain of your adolescent.

Envision yourself as an adult; comfort and soothe the pain of your adult.

Envision yourself as an elder; comfort and soothe your pain as an elder.

Close your eyes and follow through with the meditation, comforting someone else, your child, your adolescent, and yourself as an adult and an elder.

After twenty minutes slowly open your eyes and feel relaxed, repeating your mantra to yourself: compassion, compassion, compassion.

Mindful Step #2:
STOP BEING SO HARD ON YOURSELF

Goal: I will have more compassion for myself.

Mantra: ACCEPTANCE

"Progress not perfection."

—Alcholics Anonymous Proverb

You can be hard on yourself in a number of ways. You can be self-critical, expect perfection at times, and blame yourself for mistakes. However, the strongest form of self-harm is to "shame" yourself.

Shame

"Shame is a basic, natural human emotion, which in moderation is adaptive, healthy and absolutely essential for development. We could not eliminate shame even if we wanted to. It's inbred in the species."

—Edward Kaufman, from "The psychotherapy of dually diagnosed patients." *Journal of Substance Abuse Treatment*

Even though we cannot eliminate shame, we can learn how to deal with it in a more effective and mindful way. Shame is defined by Merle Fossum and Marilyn Mason in *Facing Shame* as the "self looking in on itself and finding the self lacking or flawed." Shame is often experienced publicly, causing an individual to feel exposed and vulnerable. Shameful feelings can be invoked by peers, the school system and other institutions, parents, and authority figures. Shame is also invoked by the individual. Statements such as "I should have . . ." or "Why did I . . . ?" "I am so stupid," and so on are self-shaming statements.

Shame has also been described as a flash flood of emotion that can rupture the emotional bridge in interpersonal relationships. Shame-based thoughts may literally flood the mind, disabling the individual's capacity for positive, mindful thoughts.

Shame Worsens Negative Feelings

Let's take three basic feelings—anxiety, depression, and anger—and bind or connect them to feelings of shame:

- The feelings of "anxiety plus shame" will result in cascading feelings of "panic."

- The feelings of "depression plus shame" will result in deeper feelings of "despair."
- The feelings of "anger plus shame" will result in escalating feelings of "rage."

You can see how shame escalates and cascades negative feelings, making you feel worse about yourself.

Trance of Unworthiness

In *Radical Acceptance*, Tara Brach describes shame as a "trance of unworthiness." She describes this trance as a toxic gas: "Feeling that something is wrong with me is the invisible and toxic gas I am always breathing."

Self-Compassion to Counter Shame

There is the tendency to be compassionate and understanding toward others but to not practice compassion toward ourselves. Tara Brach describes "radical acceptance" as reversing this shame-based trance of unworthiness by an inner resolve and active training of the heart and mind to recognize our true goodness.

"Lighten Up"

Life is difficult enough without beating yourself up. Give yourself a break, lighten up, and stay "in the now."

> "All beings want to be happy, yet so very few know how. It is out of ignorance that any of us cause suffering for ourselves or for others."
>
> —Sharon Salzberg, *Lovingkindness*

"It's hopeless. I'll never be able to catch my tail."

Being Mindful of "Progress Not Perfection"

The mantra "progress not perfection" needs to be a part of your mindfulness toolbox. The goal is to stay "in the now" and *be gentle with yourself*. "Progress" involves recognizing, embracing, accepting, and having compassion for your own imperfections, as well as others' imperfections. Progress means learning and moving forward.

"Radical acceptance reverses our habit of
living at war with ourselves . . . a moment of
radical acceptance is a moment of genuine freedom."

—Tara Brach, *Radical Acceptance*

Having compassion also involves self-acceptance—acceptance of what occurred in the past and openness to what is happening "in the now."

"Not harming ourselves or others
is the basis of enlightened society.
This is how there could be a sane world.
It starts with sane citizens, and that is us.
The most fundamental aggression to ourselves,
the most fundamental harm we can do to ourselves,
is to remain ignorant by not having the courage
and the respect to look at ourselves
honestly and gently."

—Pema Chodron, *Comfortable with Uncertainty*

Positive Self

Instead of being hard on yourself, focus on your positive self. A positive sense of self is when you focus on your:

- Uniqueness and worthwhileness
- Emerging talents and skills
- Ability to trust and be trusted

In *Turning the Mind Into an Ally*, Sakyong Mipham describes the positive aspects of self as:

- A stable mind
- A healthy sense of self-groundedness in the experience of basic "goodness"
- A clean view of the facts of life
- An unconditional loving heart
- The wisdom to know the right thing to do at all times

Mindful Thoughts About Self

The following examples illustrate the differences between negative self-thoughts and more mindful thoughts.

Negative self-thought—*No matter what I do, it's never going to be good enough, so why try?*

Mindful counterthought—*Stay the course.*

Doing is success. Stop being so hard on yourself. Do the best you can, and things will develop over time. Stay "in the now," and stop evaluating yourself through the eyes (judgments) of others.

Negative self-thought—*I have to be perfect to be okay.*

Mindful counterthought—*Progress not perfection.*

Just do your best and honor and affirm the progress you are making. Sometimes we get frustrated, and we need to work through those obstacles to success.

Negative self-thought—*I am afraid to make a mistake or risk failing, because if I fail I will feel shame.*

Mindful counterthought—*Mistakes are inevitable in the process of growth and learning.*

Learning from your mistakes leads to knowing yourself. Ignoring your mistakes leads to denial and delusion. Embrace your mistakes and understand yourself.

Negative self-thought—*Life is so much easier for others. Why is it so hard for me?*

Mindful counterthought—*I can honor and affirm my talents and skills.*

Some things come more easily to others. We all have unique and varied strengths and weaknesses, talents and skills.

Negative self-thought—*Look at* __________. *Now, if I could only be like that person, things would be all right.*

Mindful counterthought—*I can stay in the now and enjoy who I am.*

Everyone has problems. You may not see others' problems, and they might look good, even great, on the surface, but everyone has shortcomings.

Negative self-thought—*It's never going to get any better. Life is always going to be the same.*

Mindful counterthought—*Things change.*

Sometimes you might have to persevere longer, be more patient, but things always change. You need to be open to opportunities for growth while you are waiting for alignment.

Negative self-thought—*If only others would like me. Then I would be happy.*

Mindful counterthought—*My happiness lies within me.*

Happiness that is externally based is short-lived. Long-term happiness is not based on things, achievements, or the affirmations of others.

Mindful Activities to Stop Being So Hard on Yourself

Your Mantra Is "Acceptance"

Your mantra reminds you to accept yourself, embracing your beauty, imperfection, and uniqueness. "Acceptance" reminds you to accept your humanness with the many facets of your personality, mind, and body. Acceptance also means accepting others, seeing them as struggling with the same universal issues.

Acceptance also means seeing the good things in your life. We tend to focus on the small number of negative things about ourselves and our lives, instead of on the abundance of good things about ourselves and our lives. Accept and see the "joys" in your life and have gratitude and appreciation for what you do have.

Start your day by repeating your mantra "acceptance" in morning meditation. Remember to be gentle and accepting of yourself, your mistakes, and your imperfections, as well as the mistakes and imperfections of others.

Reread This Step to Yourself and to Others

As you did with the first mindful step, reread this step to yourself. This will keep acceptance as the focus and will remind you to invoke self-acceptance in your daily life. It is also of benefit to read this step out loud to your partner/spouse, your children, or others who are close to you.

Talents, Skills, and Self-Trust

Identify three talents and skills that you possess. Record them in your journal.

Identify three ways that you trust and can be trusted (for example: I can be relied on; I am a good friend; I have a good heart). Record them in your journal.

Walk in Nature and Affirm Yourself

Take a walk in nature by yourself. Notice your surroundings. Find an isolated spot. Sit and breathe. Listen and be quiet. Focus on the good things in your life, as well as your talents and skills. Have gratitude for your life. Let what comes flow and do not judge.

Self-Acceptance Meditation

Find a comfortable place to sit. Make yourself comfortable, on a chair or couch with your back straight and your arms resting on your lap, palms up, holding your left hand in your right palm, thumbs slightly touching.

Gently close your eyes and focus on your breath.

Breathe in slowly through your nose and exhale all your breath. Breathe in, filling your abdomen with air. Hold your breath counting to four, then exhale fully. Then breathe slowly and calmly for a few minutes.

Feel your body relax; your head is lighter; your neck has no tension. You might even want to stretch your neck from side to side, still breathing slowly.

You can relax your chest with a few deep breaths.

You can relax your belly, feeling the air fill it as you breathe in.

You can relax your hips, your butt, your legs. Feel the tension release from your legs.

You can flex and twist your feet as they relax as well.

Now slowly open your eyes and read the meditation to yourself.

Breathe. Take a deep breath and exhale slowly. Slow down and focus on your breath. Allow yourself to feel safe—safe enough to let the pain and suffering release throughout your body. Let the tears roll as they may as you let go of control.

Comfort and soothe yourself for any ordeal you have gone through. Recognize your strengths and resiliency as you imagine walking in nature, recognizing the beauty that is there and in your being.

Smile as you recognize how beautiful you are, a complicated, unique balance of qualities and features. Repeat the mantra to yourself—acceptance, acceptance, acceptance—over and over, and then say it more quietly and softly until it fades away into consciousness.

Do the same thing with the phrase "progress not perfection." Then imagine yourself going back to the beauty of nature.

Close your eyes and in your mind take a walk of self-acceptance in nature for twenty minutes. Then open your eyes feeling refreshed, with a sense of strength and goodness.

Mindful Step #3:

MAINTAIN A GOOD ATTITUDE

Goal: I will maintain a good attitude.

Mantra: ATTITUDE

We need a good attitude to break through denial, overcome delusion, and embrace discovery and change. From our youth to our old age, and every passage between, there is the need to maintain a good attitude.

Setbacks are a universal part of life. Everyone has setbacks. It is how you think and deal with these setbacks (mindfulness) that determines your ability to cope, grow, and move forward.

Having a good attitude involves having:

- Hope
- Resiliency and hardiness
- Mindful optimism

Read the following to yourself.

HOPEISNOWHERE

This is a fun exercise to bring to awareness that a slight difference in perception can lead to hope or no hope, and an optimistic or pessimistic view. In giving this exercise to numerous groups over the last few years, I have found that a majority of people see HOPE IS NOWHERE. A more optimistic view is "HOPE IS NOW HERE." (I had one person come up with the original response of HOPE I SNOW HERE. He was an avid skier and was hoping for snow!)

Western Hope and Buddhist Hope

In our Western culture, hope focuses on the future. We hope that:

- Things will get better (in the future)
- The quality of our life will improve
- Our mood will improve
- Our boredom will be relieved
- Our pains will be alleviated
- Our illness will be cured

- Our suffering will stop
- Our security will be achieved
- Our shortcomings will be fixed
- Our aloneness will be quieted
- Our death will be painless

Buddhist teachings focus on being fully present to embrace and live life with all its hardships as well as benefits with total awareness. The hope is to be fully present, living each moment of life. Mindful hope is our trust in our ability to be truly present.

Western hope is often a preoccupation with escape (escape from pain, conflict, unpleasant feelings and situations, etc.), numbing, or distracting from unpleasant feelings. Mindful hope is about staying "in the now," staying the course, and being present without delusion, distraction, and self-deception. We are mindful of our feelings, recognizing all of our feelings, both negative and positive.

In the West, our hope is often egocentric. People hope for things for themselves or for their immediate family. It was Buddha's hope to teach individuals to overcome greed, hatred, and delusion, and to develop generosity, love, and awareness. The hope was and is to develop a world of peace, tranquility, and harmony. This hope is symbolized in John Lennon's song "Imagine."

Keeping Hope Alive: "Staying the Course"

During times of personal challenge—when we become aware of the inequities in life, the discouragement when betrayed by friends/colleagues, when politics plays out to the expense of what is virtuous and right, when energy and spirit are low due to blocked goals and frustration with the incompetence of others, when the warrior's path is filled with dead ends and setbacks that erode perseverance, when motivation is low due to daily battles that sap emotional strength and mood, when strength is waning and self-doubt is rising, and when dreams and hopes are hard to maintain—these are the times we have to "stay the course," keep hope alive, and get back in touch with our heart and spirit.

Hope for Others

Along with hope for ourselves, we also need to have hope for others. Hope involves supporting and encouraging others to persevere "in the now" and to "stay the course" with integrity and virtue.

Over the last thirty years of counseling individuals with

substance abuse problems, alcoholism, drug addiction, and other related problems (trauma, violation, abandonment, family of origin issues, etc.), I have found that "hope" is the essential ingredient for recovery. The highest correlating factor that predicts success in counseling others is the counselors' belief and commitment that they will be successful in helping their clients. Staying the course with my clients, not abandoning them when they relapse, caring about their well-being, and working with them to get back on course are essential curative factors.

Resiliency and Hardiness

Having a good attitude also involves resiliency and hardiness. The capacity to overcome great adversity is labeled "resiliency." In their book *The Resilient Self,* husband and wife team Stephen Wolin, M.D., and Sybil Wolin, Ph.D., describe resilient individuals as having the insight and hope that they can make changes for a more fulfilling future.

Hardiness is another important ingredient for hope to flourish. The disposition of hardiness is described as the tendency to address stressful circumstances by:

- Accepting them as natural, even developmentally important, parts of life
- Believing one can transform them into opportunities
- Proceeding to cope decisively with them

Hardiness incorporates courage—the courage that helps people construct meaning in their lives, especially when there is emotional pain and loss. Hardy individuals confront difficult situations as a challenge and opportunity for growth.

"We who live in concentration camps can remember the men who walked through the huts comforting others, giving away their last piece of bread. They may have been few in number, but they offer sufficient proof that everything can be taken away from a man but one thing: the last of human freedoms—to choose one's attitude in any given set of circumstances, to choose one's own way."

—Viktor E. Frankl, *Man's Search for Meaning*

Optimism

Attitude, Attitude, Attitude

A good real-estate agent will tell you the best attribute of valuable property is "location, location, location." For your emotional well-being, the best attribute is attitude, attitude, attitude. People with a more positive, optimistic attitude toward life are more successful, have better relationships, and live longer, more enjoyable, and healthier lives.

Mindful Optimism

It is a mistake to label yourself as either an optimist or a pessimist. We all think both pessimistically and optimistically at various times. Pessimistic thinking frequently involves focusing on negative future outcomes rather than staying "in the now." In a similar way, optimism that involves aggrandized expectations for the future causes disappointments if those expectations are not met. Mindful optimism is about examining the way you think and avoiding negative, "knee-jerk", pessimistic reactions as well as aggrandized optimistic reactions. The key element is to be "in the now" as you work through both negative and positive experiences.

The Three P's of Pessimism

The differences between optimism and pessimism are outlined by Martin Seligman, Ph.D., in his book *Learned Optimism*. The three key elements of pessimistic thinking, outlined by Seligman, are when a person sees things as:

- Permanent
- Pervasive
- Personal

"The defining characteristics of pessimists is that they tend to believe bad events will last a long time, will undermine everything they do, and are their own fault."

—Martin Seligman, *Learned Optimism*

The three key elements of optimism are when an individual interprets and sees things as:

- Very temporary
- Specific
- External

Very Temporary Instead of Permanent

"The optimist tends to believe defeat
is just a temporary setback, that its causes
are confined to one case, and it
(defeat) is not their fault."

—Martin Seligman, *Learned Optimism*

A pessimist believes that bad events will last a long time—that they have permanence. The *permanent* thoughts that "nothing will change" and "I will be stuck in this state of discomfort and depression forever" are the thoughts of the pessimist. The depressed and pessimistic mind is like a runaway freight train headed for an inevitable crash. The mind needs to hit the brakes and sagely slow down to see the true reality (that most of these things are temporary, and there is a better way of responding and coping) to avoid the emotional train wreck.

Specific Instead of Pervasive

"Finding temporary and specific causes
for misfortune is the art of hope."

—Martin Seligman, *Learned Optimism*

Optimistic thinking involves accepting mistakes and seeing them as being related to a specific issue. It involves recognizing that the problem is specific and not generalized to many aspects of our lives.

External Instead of Personalized

"Shit happens."

—Alcoholics Anonymous Proverb

Pessimistic thinking personalizes setbacks, even when the setback is something that is out of our control (external). You are not the center of the universe. You are in life with others, and sometimes you get the short end of the stick. We need to learn not to personalize situations that don't meet our needs and expectations, and to recognize they are external and often out of our control.

Mindful Activities for Maintaining a Good Attitude

Your Mantra Is "Attitude"

Remember that your mantra for this step is "attitude." Invoke your mantra to remind yourself to be "hopeful" toward your own situation as well as toward others. You can start your day by repeating your mantra "attitude" in morning meditation. When conflict arises, invoke the mantra "attitude." Maintain optimism "in the now," and remember that no one knows what tomorrow will bring. Avoid seeing things as personal, pervasive, and permanent. Be open to discovery and change.

Reread This Step to Yourself and to Others

As you did with the previous mindful steps, reread this step to yourself. This will keep hope and mindful optimism as the focus and will remind you to invoke hope and mindful optimism in your daily life. It is also beneficial to read this step out loud to your partner/spouse, your children, or others who are close to you, especially during times of conflict and challenge.

What Helps You to Have Hope?

In your journal, identify all of the sources of hope that apply to you and add any other sources of hope that you might have.

- My religion
- My faith

- My relationship with my family
- My children
- My belief in myself
- My work
- My spirituality
- My contribution to others' lives
- My ability to learn and grow
- My relationships with others
- My joy in nature
- My belief in the goodness of others

In your journal, explain how these sources of hope help you.

Rate Your Overall Level of Optimism

On a scale of 1 to 7 (1 = very low, 7 = very high) rate your overall level of optimism and answer the questions that follow in your journal.

- What are you pessimistic about?
- Are these things you need to be pessimistic about? Explain.
- Who might you talk to, to help you worry less and be less pessimistic and more optimistic?
- What can you do to be less pessimistic and more optimistic?

Write Your Own Eulogy

What do you want people to say about you when you die? Record it in your journal.

Attitude Meditation

Find a comfortable place to sit. Make yourself comfortable, on a chair or couch with your back straight and your arms resting on your lap, palms up, holding your left hand in your right palm, thumbs slightly touching.

Gently close your eyes and focus on your breath.

Breathe in slowly through your nose and exhale all your breath. Breathe in, filling your abdomen with air. Hold your breath counting to four, then exhale fully. Then breathe slowly and calmly for a few minutes.

Feel your body relax; your head is lighter; your neck has no tension. You might even want to stretch your neck from side to side, still breathing slowly.

You can relax your chest with a few deep breaths.

You can relax your belly, feeling the air fill it as you breathe in.

You can relax your hips, your butt, your legs. Feel the tension release from your legs.

You can flex and twist your feet as they relax as well.

Now slowly open your eyes and read the meditation to yourself.

I recognize how my attitude strongly influences the way I approach life and others. I can focus on my goodness and wholeheartedness.

Close your eyes, reflect, and meditate for twenty minutes on an attitude of hope, peace, optimism, tranquility, and compassion.

Mindful Step #4:
OPEN UP TO "DISCOVERY"

Goal: I will avoid denial and self-delusion and be open to discovery.

Mantra: DISCOVERY

Denial and Self-Delusion

The old joke in the alcohol/drug recovery field was that denial was a river in Egypt (de Nile). A more contemporary description of "D-E-N-I-A-L" is: **I** "**D**on't **E**ven k**N**ow **I** **A**m **L**ying." Denial is a way of protecting the ego from being hurt. There are many ways that people maintain denial and self-delusion (see "Denial Defense Mechanism" on page 74). The result is the same—a self-delusion about what is reality.

DENIAL DEFENSE MECHANISMS

Rationalizations—Reasons that justify maintaining unhealthy behaviors. "It is not that bad."

Minimizations—Discounting the negative consequences of unhealthy behaviors. "My problems are really not that significant."

Othering—Comparing negative behaviors and consequences to someone who has more dramatic negative behaviors and consequences. "Now look at so and so; he/she really has a problem."

Forms of Procrastination—Waiting to change negative behaviors at a later date. "I will do it later when it is more convenient."

Breaking Through Denial and Delusion: Opening Up to Discovery

Living a life in fear of loss will create a "fearful and lost life." Living a life of control and rigidity will create a life that is "closed and static."

"We move through the world in a narrow groove,
preoccupied with the petty things we see and hear,
brooding over our prejudices, passing by the joys of life
without even knowing that we have missed anything.
Never for a moment do we taste the heady wine of
freedom. We are as truly imprisoned as if we lay at
the bottom of a dungeon, heaped with chains."

—Yang Chu, fourth century BCE Chinese philosopher
(in Steve Hagen, *Buddhism Plain and Simple*)

Opening up to discovery means looking at things with openness and seeing them as they really are. It requires the ability to accept and work through difficult times, make healthy changes, and embrace personal growth.

"The essence of bravery is being
without self-deception."

—Pema Chodron, *The Places That Scare You*

Opening up to discovery invites awareness and possibility of living life fully, being present in each moment, and embracing personal freedom.

Johari Window: A Tool for Self-Discovery

The Johari Window is not some magical construct developed in India. It was actually developed by two trainers/coaches named Joe and Harry, hence Joe-Harry to Johari. It has been used for many years as a teaching tool to help you understand what you know and don't know about yourself. The Johari Window illustrates four categories of self, as shown in the diagram below. These categories are:

The public self—things you know that others know.

The private self—things you know that others don't know.

The blind self—things you don't know that others know.

The discovery self—things you don't know that others don't know.

		You	
		Know	**Don't Know**
OTHERS	**Know**	Public Self	Blind Self
	Don't Know	Private Self	Discovery Self

TAPE IN MIDDLE; DO NOT STAPLE

NO POSTAGE
NECESSARY
IF MAILED
IN THE
UNITED STATES

BUSINESS REPLY MAIL

FIRST-CLASS MAIL PERMIT NO 45 DEERFIELD BEACH, FL

POSTAGE WILL BE PAID BY ADDRESSEE

Health Communications, Inc.
3201 SW 15th Street
Deerfield Beach FL 33442-9875

FOLD HERE

Comments

There are things that you know about yourself that others know; this is called the "public self." This would include general, publicly accessible information.

The "private self" includes those things that you know about yourself that others don't know. Of course, this would include intimate and personal information that you choose to keep private.

The "blind self" includes those things that you don't know about yourself that others know about you.

The "discovery self" refers to the opportunities that arise when both you and others don't know things about you. Through exploration, you discover something that you and others were not aware of previously. This is a very exciting area of life in which you can experience a journey of self-discovery.

Blocks to Discovery

Stuck in Your Own Head

Discovery is often blocked by preconceived notions, biases, and judgments. If you are stuck in your head, you aren't listening to your heart—a heart that has empathy, compassion, and connection.

"Men are afraid to forget their minds,
fearing to fall through the Void with nothing
to stay their fall. They do not know that the Void
is not really void, but the realm of the real Dharma."

—Huang Po (in Mark Epstein,
Going to Pieces Without Falling Apart)

Racing Thought Streams

Thinking too much is an affliction of the mind. These racing thought streams block mindfulness, making it difficult for you to be "in the now." Metaphorically, obsessive thinking is like a toilet that is broken and the water is continuously running. The noise of the running water is so extremely annoying that you are unable to concentrate and discovery is blocked.

DISCOVERY

Open your mind to discovery by:

- Being open to seeing your own denial and delusions
- Putting aside your biases and judgments
- Slowing down "racing thought streams"
- Opening your heart while calming your thoughts
- Having full attention while being relaxed
- Smiling when you discover your own "blind spots"

Denial—Making the Best Choices

There are pivotal times in our lives when one choice may lead to incredibly positive change and another choice might lead to negative, even catastrophic results. These decision points are crossroads where denial and self-delusion come into play. The following true story illustrates this point.

True Story: Mother Love Bone to Pearl Jam

Andy Wood was the lead singer for Mother Love Bone, a Seattle-based grunge rock band. Andy was referred to me by a former client who cared greatly about him.

I knew nothing about the band or the grunge scene, but I was intrigued by Andy's situation. The band had been doing very well locally, and the promise of a big recording contract with a high-profile Los Angeles–based label was close at hand.

At our first session I found Andy to be soft spoken, sweet, and very amiable, quite in contrast with his stage persona. Andy quickly acknowledged that he had a heroin addiction. He immediately agreed to go to a residential (inpatient) drug-treatment program.

I had the initial feeling that Andy's underlying shy personality was in conflict with the demands of his performance persona and the responsibility of being the lead singer. Of course, there would be even more pressure as the band was becoming more than just a local favorite. However, I would never have the chance to find out if my feeling was accurate or not.

Andy successfully completed drug treatment and was staying sober. I was seeing him on an outpatient basis a couple of times a week, and he was doing very well. He was more alive and fun loving and was enjoying himself. This was quite the contrast from his deadened, numb personality when he was using heroin. Things were going well in his life. He was 100 days sober, and the band and other people close to him were very proud of him.

Unfortunately, many relapses occur when people are doing well and begin to underestimate the power of addiction. The majority of relapses occur within the first 30 to 180 days of sobriety. I am sure Andy's decisions to use heroin was spontaneous—an impulsive decision (*brain* not *mind* decision). A fan gave Andy some really pure heroin. I can imagine that Andy's addict brain was in denial, thinking:

What's the harm?

It is free.

I can do just a little bit.

Here it is—I didn't go looking for it.

Who will know?

Any number of denial rationalizations were possible, rather than more mindful thinking:

I am a recovering heroin addict, and I can't even do a little of this or any other drug, including alcohol.

Drugs can kill me, especially this drug.

I haven't used in one hundred days. I don't want to lose that sobriety, and my tolerance is so low I might overdose.

In reality that is what happened. The combination of Andy's low tolerance after one 100 clean days and the high purity of the heroin were deadly. The drug and his addiction killed Andy Wood. That is what I said in my eulogy at his funeral at the Paramount Theater in Seattle, a few days after his death.

After Andy's death the band hooked up with a new lead singer, Eddie Vedder. They landed a record contract, and they were on their way.

A few years later I happened across an issue of *Time* magazine that was delivered to my counseling office. Pearl Jam was on the front cover. They had become the most popular and successful grunge band ever.

Unfortunately, this true story points out the thin line between a path of success and a path of failure and death. Andy died of a drug overdose, never to realize his life's ambition. The band goes on to unlimited success, fulfilling the dreams of its members.

Mindful Activities for Discovery

Your Mantra Is "Discovery"

Your mantra reminds you to avoid denial and delusion and to be open to discovery. Start your day by repeating your mantra "discovery" in morning meditation.

Reread This Step to Yourself and to Others

As you did with the previous mindful steps, reread this step to yourself. This will keep "discovery" as the focus and will remind you to invoke discovery in your daily life. It is also of benefit to read this step out loud to your partner/spouse, your children, or others who are close to you.

Discovery: Thinking Outside of the Box

Opening up to discovery involves "thinking outside of the box." I encourage you to expand your consciousness by developing a mind that is open to thinking outside of the box but also integrates what you know about yourself. Many people are natural "out of the box" thinkers. When someone tells them they can't do something or it is impossible, they are not deterred. Instead, they become more determined and focused on finding a way to be successful.

Discovery is a natural part of their lives; creativity and challenge are what they thrive on. They have passion and motivation to question their own feelings, motives, and desires and to go further than others who might doubt them. Of course, a truly mindful person will also consider his or her own blind spots and denial.

Try using "out of the box" thinking to complete the following puzzle. Connect the nine dots with four straight lines, without picking up your pen from the paper.

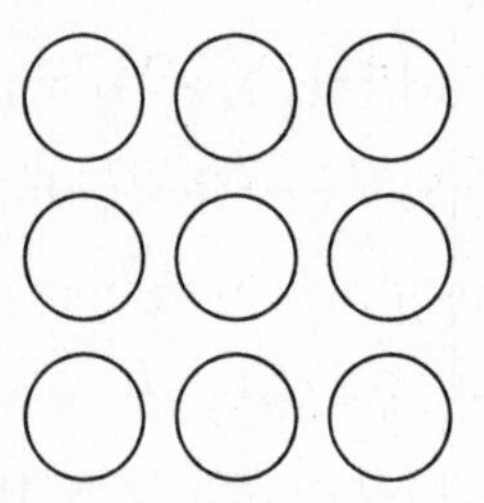

Try again, if you were not successful. The solution can be found on page 88.

By going out of the mindset of the box, the puzzle can be solved. Metaphorically, thinking "outside of the box" is often necessary to solve the problems of life.

Read About Mindfulness and Self-Discovery

Select one of the books from the Reference section on page 173, and read about mindfulness. Write down any insights about yourself as a result of reading, and share that with someone close to you.

Act

Take a class, workshop, and/or retreat that promotes self-discovery and mindfulness.

Ask for Help!

Ask for help from a counselor, a trusted teacher or spiritual leader, a close friend, or a partner/spouse to help you identify things you might be in denial about and possibilities that you might be ignoring.

Follow Through

Take "action" by taking steps toward addressing denial and embracing discovery. Describe what you are going to do in your journal.

Discovery Meditation

Find a comfortable place to sit. Make yourself comfortable, on a chair or couch with your back straight and your arms resting on your lap, palms up, holding your left hand in your right palm, thumbs slightly touching.

Gently close your eyes and focus on your breath.

Breathe in slowly through your nose and exhale all your breath. Breathe in, filling your abdomen with air. Hold your breath counting to four, then exhale fully. Then breathe slowly and calmly for a few minutes.

Feel your body relax; your head is lighter; your neck has no tension. You might even want to stretch your neck from side to side, still breathing slowly.

You can relax your chest with a few deep breaths.

You can relax your belly, feeling the air fill it as you breathe in.

You can relax your hips, your butt, your legs. Feel the tension release from your legs.

You can flex and twist your feet as they relax as well.

Now slowly open your eyes and read the meditation to yourself.

Imagine yourself going on a journey of discovery.

You are a young child, and you have a friend who is about the same age. You are on a beach, and you both slip into the water.

You go under the water and are able to breathe in the water like a fish, and your feet have turned into fins. You are joyful and carefree as you and your friend frolic in the water, twisting and turning with your newfound aquatic capabilities.

Laughing at your new freedom, you swim with a variety of colorful fish.

A pod of dolphins beckon you from a distance. You stare at them momentarily, as they encourage you to join them. In a flicker, you both join them, swimming, jumping, and laughing at the sheer joy of it all.

They lead you to a deserted island, giving you a little nudge as you swim ashore. As you touch land, your fins turn back into feet, and you slowly walk out of the surf. The dolphins are gone. You and your friend are on the long, white deserted beach as the waves slap quietly at the shore.

Close your eyes, imagine taking your friend's hand, and go on a journey of discovery. After twenty minutes, swim with the dolphins back to your starting point.

Open your eyes, and journal what happened as a keepsake of your "discovery" experience.

Solution to the puzzle:

By going out of the mind set of the box, the puzzle is able to be solved. Metaphorically, thinking "outside of the box" is often necessary to solve the problems of life.

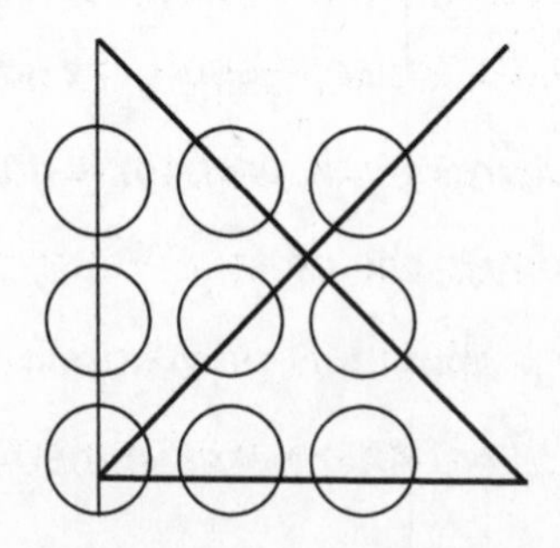

Mindful Step #5:

EMBRACE POSITIVE AND HEALTHY CHANGE

Goal: I will deal with those things that block positive and healthy change.

Mantra: CHANGE

Change: A Multifaceted Concept

The whole concept of change is fascinating and very complicated. People change for a variety of personal and individual reasons. Change can take a long time to occur or seem like a spontaneous decision. Many people can go for years, even a lifetime, wanting to change something about their lives or themselves, but avoid making the change. They may frequently verbalize a desire and need to change, saying they will change, yet they maintain the status quo. Other individuals may not say a word about making a change, then just wake up one morning and take action. It may appear like a spontaneous decision to change, but in actuality it probably was a long time in coming.

Others Influence Change

"Motivation is a state of readiness or eagerness to change, which may fluctuate from one time to another. This state is one that can be influenced."

—William Miller and Stephen Rollnick, *Motivational Interviewing*

The motivation to change is a state of mind. Others influence this change state of mind directly and indirectly. Friends, teachers, family members, mentors, and others can help you see the need for change and help support that change. Certainly counselors are helpful change agents.

Hearing the same thing from different people, in a timely manner, may cause you to consider making a change. Sometimes a heartstring is touched or a sign may awaken an individual to an insight that change is needed. There is a Buddhist proverb that compares change to tuning a guitar. If the strings are too tight, or too lose, you can't make music.

Issues of Surrender and Control

Change is described as "mindful surrender" or an acceptance that efforts to control an "outcome" may actually be out of our control. Sometimes it is only when we truly let go that things can change.

"Giving up control—often we are afraid of falling apart, but the problem is that we have not learned how to give up control of ourselves. Buddhism recognizes that the central issues of our lives, from falling in love to facing death, require an ability to surrender that often eludes us."

—Mark Epstein, *Going to Pieces Without Falling Apart*

The Serenity Prayer of Alcoholics Anonymous is a good way to remind yourself that you are not always in control.

SERENITY PRAYER

God grant me the serenity
To accept the things I cannot change,
The courage to change the things I can,
And the wisdom to know the difference.

Accepting the things I cannot change means accepting what can't be controlled or is out of our sphere of influence. It also means accepting life situations that may be unjust or unfair or not what we wanted but are out of our control.

The courage to change the things I can means addressing and acting on the positive and healthy things that we can change. This involves personal, interpersonal, and spiritual growth.

And the wisdom to know the difference means learning to identify what is "in" and "out" of our control. We need to let those things out of our control run their course. We can then identify when and how we can influence these events toward a more positive and healthier resolution.

Another, more personalized version of the Serenity Prayer is:

> Grant me the serenity
> to accept the people I cannot change,
> The courage to change the one I can,
> And the wisdom to know it's me.

What Blocks Change?

We block change. We might blame circumstances, other people, or the past, but the real block to change is our sense of inadequacy that feeds our fears. The reality is that freedom is ours to take. Tara Brach says it well in *Radical Acceptance*: "The biggest tragedy in our lives is that freedom is possible, yet we can pass our years trapped in the same old patterns. Entangled in the trance of unworthiness, we grow accustomed to encaging ourselves in with self-judgment and anxiety, with restlessness and dissatisfaction." If we wait too long to change, we lose our ability to be alive and enjoy life. Brach illustrates this idea with this touching story about the tiger Mohini:

> Mohini was a regal white tiger who lived for many years at the Washington, D.C., National Zoo. For most of those years her home was in the old lion house—a typical twelve-by-twelve foot cage with iron bars and a cement floor. Mohini spent her days pacing restlessly back and forth in her cramped quarters.
>
> Eventually, biologists and staff worked together to create a natural habitation for her. Converting several acres, it had hills, trees, a pond and a variety of vegetation. With excitement and anticipation they released Mohini into her new and expansive environment. But it was too late. The tiger immediately sought refuge in a corner off the compound, where she lived for the remainder of her life. Mohini paced and paced in that

corner until an area twelve-by-twelve feet was worn bare of grass."

This story reminds us to not wait too long to make positive and healthy changes. If we wait too long, we might not be able to change and will miss out on the opportunities for self-growth and new discoveries.

Here are some major factors that block positive and healthy change:

- Procrastination
- Rejection sensitivity
- Poor frustration tolerance
- Unresolved grief
- Chaos

Procrastination

"I have often thought about conducting
a seminar on the topic of procrastination,
but I put it off because I thought
no one would show up."

—Richard Fields

Procrastination is the number-one reason people do not implement change. We all procrastinate about something, whether it is taking out the garbage or completing an important task. The real issue is the cost of procrastination. When the cost of procrastination outweighs the benefits, it is time to do something. Being aware of the costs of procrastination is often a first step in readiness for change.

Linda Sapadin and Jack Maguire outline six styles of procrastination in their book *It's About Time: The Six Styles of Procrastination and How to Overcome Them.* I have adapted their descriptions of procrastination here.

1. **The Perfectionist Procrastinator.** The perfectionist procrastinator waits and waits for the perfect time and situation to take action and misses out on the opportunities for growth.
2. **The Dreamer Procrastinator.** Dreamer procrastinators (the "talkers") have unrealistic expectations. They talk about what they are going to do but take little action toward those dreams ("One day I am going to . . .").
3. **The Worrier Procrastinator.** The worrier procrastinator comes up with fearful reasons for not taking action.
4. **The Defier Procrastinator.** The defier procrastinator doesn't follow good advice, doesn't ask for help, and continues to experience the same problems.

5. **The Crisis-Maker Procrastinator.** Crisis-maker procrastinators create crises to distract from taking "right action." They are drama prone. They are so busy putting out fires that they avoid working on the real issues.
6. **The Overdoer Procrastinator.** The overdoer procrastinator will focus on one part of a problem at the expense of taking up the priority issues.

Rejection Sensitivity

Learning to tolerate rejection can help us to move forward and overcome procrastination. Being aware that rejection is a part of life and not overreacting to rejection can be accomplished by invoking the awareness of "progress not perfection."

Poor Frustration Tolerance

When goals are blocked, or there are setbacks in relationships or life, individuals get frustrated. Being able to persevere through adversity and having tolerance for frustrating situations is necessary for healthy change to take place. In order to embrace healthy change, we also need to have the ability to slow down and to be more patient. We need to recognize that "progress is slow" and "patience is a virtue."

"Time is a flying bird. Do you want to capture
the bird and encage it? Then you need patience.
Your fondest dreams will be transformed into fruitful
realities if you just know the secret of
growing the patience-tree in your heart."

—Sri Chinmoy, *The Wisdom of Sri Chinmoy*

Unresolved Grief: Getting Unstuck

People resist change when they have not adequately worked through loss. They are stuck living in the past loss, unable to stay "in the now."

Elisabeth Kübler-Ross, in *On Death and Dying*, her groundbreaking work with clients who were dying, identified five stages of grieving:

- Denial
- Anger
- Bargaining
- Depression
- Acceptance

To grieve, an individual needs to break through denial, deal with anger and resentments, overcome unhealthy unrealistic bargains, deal with the feelings, and embrace acceptance.

Chaos

All of these factors—procrastination, rejection sensitivity, poor frustration tolerance, and unresolved grief—contribute to "chaos" in our personal and professional lives. Chaos can take many forms, from the garage, the house, and the office that are a "mess," to the missed appointments and mismanagement of personal and professional projects. Chaos distracts from mindfulness, as the brain is cluttered with unresolved issues and overwhelmed with too much information. Chaos causes us to avoid responsibility and distracts from clarity. In chaos, the waters of life are so muddy that we cannot make clear decisions until we clean up the murkiness.

Exertion: An Essential Element of Change

Overcoming these obstacles to change requires effort, exertion, and commitment. This is described quite clearly by Pema Chodron in *When Things Fall Apart*: Exertion is "like waking up on a cold, snowy day in a mountain cabin ready to go for a walk but knowing that you have to get out of bed and make a fire. You'd rather stay in bed, but you jump out and make the fire because the brightness of the day is bigger than staying in bed."

The Spiral of Change—Stages of Change

William Miller, lead author of *Motivational Interviewing*, describes change as a process with specific stages that can be influenced.

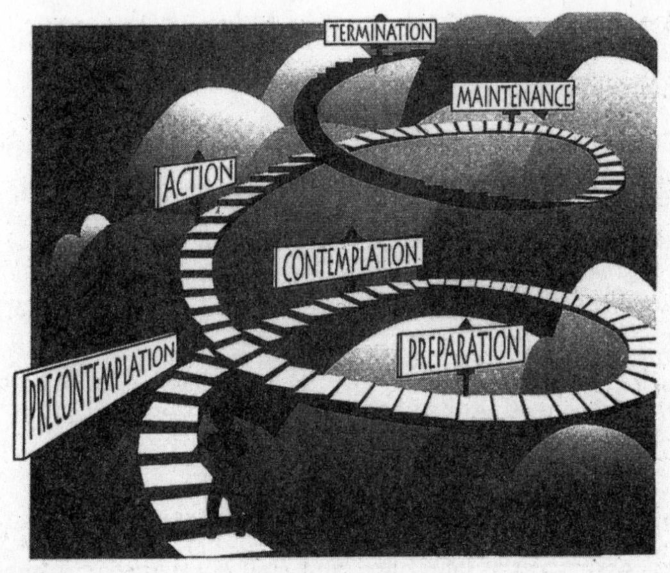

5.1 Spiral of Change

Precontemplative stage—At this stage you are not entertaining the idea of change. You may be maintaining unhealthy behaviors and ignoring or denying the need to change. You will move toward readiness for contemplation of change when you begin to see the risks and problems in not making a change.

Contemplative stage—At this stage you are thinking about (contemplating) positive change but are experiencing a great deal of ambivalence. You can influence change at this stage by exploring the pros and cons of ambivalence. If you can identify what the roadblocks to change are and the price to be paid by procrastinating, that can also influence change.

Determination stage—At this stage you have committed to change. You need to determine the best way to proceed for effective healthy change.

Action stage—At this stage you are taking action and implementing your plan for change. You need to deal with your remaining feelings of ambivalence in order to completely follow through with action.

Maintenance stage—This stage involves doing what is necessary on a daily basis and being aware of potential relapses.

Relapse prevention stage—At this stage, situations, thoughts, behaviors, triggers, and cravings that may cause relapse back to the old unhealthy behavior need to be addressed. Continued vigilance will be necessary to avoid relapse, especially when in a vulnerable state (see HALTS in Mindful Step # 7).

Quantum Change

Change does not always go through the stages described; people can skip stages. In their book *Quantum Change: When Epiphanies and Sudden Insights Transform Ordinary Lives,* William Miller and coauthor Janet C'de Baca describe a more sudden and immediate kind of change as "quantum change." A quantum change is described as a *personal transformation* that has some key elements in being:

Vivid—Identifiable, distinctive experiences during which the transformation occurred or at least began.

Surprising—Not comprehensible as ordinary response to life events.

Benevolent—Involves loving-kindness.

Enduring—A permanent transformation.

Involved in conflict—A rupture in the knowing context. Miller and C'de Baca quote Bill W., the cofounder of Alcoholics Anonymous, as he describes his quantum change: "Slowly the ecstasy subsided. I lay on the bed, but know for a time I was in another world, a new world of consciousness. All about me and through me there was a wonderful feeling of presence. A great peace stole over me and I thought 'No matter how wrong things seem to be, they are all right.'"

Mindful Activities for Change

Your Mantra Is "Change"

Invoking your mantra of change reminds you to overcome the blocks to change and to exert yourself. Your mantra can help to move you to decide to make some changes and to maintain change. When change is difficult, invoke the mantra "change" to fight the temptation to give up, regress, or relapse. Start your day by repeating your mantra "change" in morning meditation. Repeat the mantra over and over when addressing obstacles to change.

Reread This Step to Yourself and to Others

As you did with the previous mindful steps, reread this step to yourself. This will keep change as the focus and will remind you to invoke change in your daily life.

It is also of benefit to read this step out loud to your partner/spouse, your children, or others who are close to you.

Make One Change

1. Identify one change you would like to make and record it in your journal.
2. What stage of change are you currently at in relation to the change you wish to make?
   - Precontemplative
   - Contemplative
   - Determination
   - Action
   - Maintenance
   - Relapse prevention
3. Rate your motivation to make this change on a scale of 0 to 10 (0 = not motivated at all; 10 = highly motivated).
4. List any benefits that you might have for maintaining the problematic behavior. List all the reasons for not changing, until you can't think of any more.

5. List as many negative consequences of and drawbacks to not making this change as you can think of.
6. What may block your desire to change? Record all that apply.
   - Procrastination
   - Rejection Sensitivity
   - Poor Frustration Tolerance
   - Unresolved grief
   - Chaos
7. Rank those blocks to change, from strongest to weakest.
8. What action are you going to take to overcome any of these blocks?
9. Identify two people who will support your change.
10. Ask those two people for help in implementing the change!

Change Meditation

Find a comfortable place to sit. Make yourself comfortable, on a chair or couch with your back straight and your arms resting on your lap, palms up, holding your left hand in your right palm, thumbs slightly touching.

Gently close your eyes and focus on your breath.

Breathe in slowly through your nose and exhale all your breath. Breathe in, filling your abdomen with air. Hold your breath counting to four, then exhale fully. Then breathe slowly and calmly for a few minutes.

Feel your body relax; your head is lighter; your neck has no tension. You might even want to stretch your neck from side to side, still breathing slowly.

You can relax your chest with a few deep breaths.

You can relax your belly, feeling the air fill it as you breathe in.

You can relax your hips, your butt, and your legs. Feel the tension release from your legs.

You can flex and twist your feet as they relax as well.

Now slowly open your eyes and read the meditation to yourself.

I recognize that change is a natural part of life.

I will work through my feelings of ambivalence about healthy and positive change.

I will seek help and direction from others who have the ability to not only motivate healthy and positive change, but can also provide information, advice, and support.

I realize that it is my own procrastination and the chaos that I create in my own life that most often blocks change.

I know that progress is often slow, and patience is a virtue.

I no longer resist positive and healthy change, as I work through the stages of change.

Close your eyes and spend the next twenty minutes imagining a positive and healthy change in your life. When you are done, journal what that change looked and felt like.

Section Two: Enhancement

Mindful Step #6:
STAY "IN THE NOW"

Goal: I will stay "in the now" and dispute distorted realities that may lead to anxiety and depression.

Mantra: NOW

Staying "in the Now"

"Find the narrow gate that leads to life.
It is called the NOW."
—Eckhart Tolle, *The Power of Now*

Throughout this book I have been using the phrase "staying in the now." Overreacting to situations instead of staying "in the now" can lead to escalated feelings of anxiety and depression. "Anxiety" is defined as vague fear—an expectation that something is going to go wrong, but not knowing exactly what. Depression has as a key element poor future orientation—expecting that the future is going to be bad.

Focusing on the past often involves preoccupation with loss, missed opportunities, shame, betrayal, and other negative emotions. A better approach is to **accept the past and move on to commitments "in the now."**

> "You can certainly learn from past experiences and mistakes, and that is valuable. But most people instead focus on their failures, their wounds, and their own personal inadequacy."
>
> — Donald Rothberg, *The Engaged Spiritual Life*

It is "What if?" future thinking that causes people to overthink things that they may never have to worry about.

What if something goes wrong?
What if I am disappointed?
What if it doesn't happen?
What if it does happen?

Jack Kornfield describes love of the past as memory and love of the future as the dream. He describes a friend who saw a sign in a Las Vegas casino that epitomizes staying "in the now." The sign read: MUST BE PRESENT TO WIN.

Disputing Distorted Realities

Instead of focusing on ruminative anxiety and obsessive "wandering attention" (depression), I encourage you to dispute these distorted realities. The key is to accept those things that are occurring "in the now," and commit to do something about them. Thinking can become an obsessive, automatic, compulsive, even addicting pattern. Thinking that results in a repetitive, obsessive preoccupation in a vicious cycle of negative and fear-based thoughts prevents you from staying "in the now." Much of counseling is pointing out to clients that this compulsive pattern of thinking is doing more harm than good.

Our functional definition of addiction involves the three *C*'s:

- **C**ompulsion/obsession
- Inability to **C**ontrol
- Continued use despite negative **C**onsequences

Thinking can clearly meet this definition of addiction. Compulsive thinking is when you are unable to stop ruminative thought streams and continue to "loop" the same thoughts over and over like an old 45 rpm record that is stuck, playing the same tune over and over.

"I would say about 80 to 90 percent
of most people's thinking is not only repetitive
and useless, but because of its dysfunctional
and often negative nature, much of it is also harmful.
Observe your mind and you will find this to be true.
It causes a serious leakage of vital energy."

—Eckhart Tolle, *The Power of Now*

Mindful thinking is not getting lost in your thoughts. Mindful thinking is more focused and involves concentrating on what you can do "in the now." Mindfulness involves being present in the moment, living life.

"Have the courage to live and enjoy
in the now, and the gratitude for what is."

—Donald Rothberg, *The Engaged Spiritual Life*

Dispute the Distorted Reality of Anxiety: Organizing Your Fear

"Nothing to fear but fear itself."

—Winston Churchill

The natural, primary "fight or flight" response to fear is wired to activate a variety of physiological systems (increased heart rate, shortness of breath, sweating). Anxiety is, metaphorically, like a smoke alarm that goes off when there is no fire.

The famous British stage actor Sir Alec Guinness suffered from panic attacks in the form of "stage fright." When asked by a critic if he still got butterflies in his stomach before each performance, he responded in his upper-crust British accent: "My good man, I still get butterflies in my stomach . . . but now they fly in formation!"

What Sir Alec had discovered was that he was busy thinking about all the possible things that could go wrong (forgetting his lines, falling down, etc.). His brain would respond by producing panic physiological responses. Sir Alec had learned to give his mind more strength. He learned to slow his breathing and relax to calm himself and the anxiety-based physiological responses. His mind then put his fears into reality by organizing his thoughts and having the butterflies "fly in formation."

Mind over Mood: Overcoming Depression

"Depression is a disorder of conscious thought."

—Aaron Beck, *Depression*

Depression shuts down the energy systems that fuel the power of the mind. The signs of depression are physical and psychological and are what therapists refer to as the "vegetative signs of depression" (see page 115). "Vegetative" is an appropriate and descriptive label, as depression is, metaphorically, like being a vegetable, just sitting there vegetating, although some of my clients describe themselves as feeling like a "wet noodle." Whether you feel like a wet noodle or a vegetable, the experience of feeling depressed is not fun.

VEGETATIVE SIGNS OF DEPRESSION

Anergia—Lack of energy; you don't have the energy to do things that you normally enjoyed doing, and normal tasks of life (doing the laundry, cleaning, etc.) are even harder to do.

Anhedonia—Lack of pleasure for things that were normally pleasurable; things that you liked to do seem to have lost their enjoyment.

Concentration—Difficulty concentrating; difficulty remembering things.

Sex Drive—Reduced, nonexistent, or increased sex drive.

Sleep—Difficulty sleeping, complaining about being tired because of poor sleep, or sleeping excessively.

Appetite—Increased appetite, or inability to eat.

Fatigue—Excessive feelings of being tired and a general "malaise."

The brain can become cemented on the thought that the future is going to continue to be filled with depression and self-doubt, and there is no way out. Those depressed rigidly adhere to the belief that they will stay in depression, that they can't see a way to overcome their depression or a better, more enjoyable life in the future.

Christine Padesky, Ph.D., coauthor of *Mind Over Mood*, says that the first step in overcoming depression is to "dispute the distorted reality."

"The clear nature of our mind is always there,
waiting to be revealed when the clouds
of the disturbing attitudes are dispelled."
—Thubten Chodren, *Open Heart, Clear Mind*

Depression as the Eeyore Syndrome

The donkey, Eeyore, in the children's book *Winnie-the-Pooh*, could be clinically described as suffering from depression. When Eeyore is asked by Pooh and other characters in the story, "Would you like to go swimming today?" Eeyore answers, in his low, monotone, depressed voice with a number of negative (vegetative) statements:

"No, I'm so tired today."

"It's too far to walk to the swimming hole."

"I might get sunburned on a sunny day like today."

"It's too hot and I might get overheated."

Eeyore worries about everything. He misses out on opportunities to enjoy himself and others. Instead of enjoying the activity (swimming) and a beautiful summer day, he isolates himself. He worries instead about potential problems. He has trouble enjoying life and staying "in the now."

Distracting from Negative, Depressive Thinking

The next step in overcoming depressive thinking is to distract from the negative thoughts. For example, the depressive thinker needs to get his or her body moving. The body and mind need a "jump-start," like a car that isn't able to run because the battery is weak or dead. The individual tries to turn on the mind to a different way of thinking, but it needs a charge—not a large one, just enough positive electrical juice to get the mindful engine to turn over. The charge in this case is physical movement.

I jokingly tell my clients who think depressively to start

using LSD. They look at me as if I am nuts. Having gotten their attention, I then explain to them that I am not talking about the hallucinogen LSD, but instead "**l**ong, **s**low, **d**istance" walking or jogging. Like the car that has a weak battery, you need to recharge your battery (mind) and get the engine (body) running so that the other systems can function more effectively.

So the first step is to get out the door, regardless of the weather, and walk for forty-five minutes or longer.

STAYING "IN THE NOW"

Mindful Step #6 involves:

- Staying "in the now" instead of having anxiety- and depressive-based thoughts about the past and future
- Recognizing that anxiety and depression are thought disorders
- Organizing your thoughts and "disputing distorted realities"
- "Distracting" from anxious and depressive thoughts
- Exercising—**L**ong, **s**low, **d**istance (LSD) walking or other forms of exercise (see Mindful Step #8: Embrace Healthy Habits—Exercise and Flow)

Mindful Activities for Staying "in the Now"

Your Mantra Is "Now"

Repeat your mantra "now" to remind yourself to stay in the present and to short-circuit feelings of anxiety and depression. When anxiety or depression comes up, repeat the mantra over and over to yourself to help you focus on being in life and doing what you can moment to moment, a day at a time. Start your day by repeating your mantra "now" in morning meditation.

Reread This Step to Yourself and to Others

As you did with the previous mindful steps, reread this step to yourself. This will keep "now" as the focus and will remind you to stay "in the now" in your daily life. It is also of beneficial to read this step out loud to your partner/spouse, your children, or others who are close to you.

Staying "in the Now" Meditation

Find a comfortable place to sit. Make yourself comfortable, sitting in a chair or couch with your back straight and your arms resting on your lap, palms up, holding your left hand in your right palm, thumbs slightly touching.

Gently close your eyes and focus on your breath.

Breathe in slowly through your nose and exhale all of your breath. Breathe in, filling your abdomen with air. Hold your breath counting to four, then exhale fully. Then breathe slowly and calmly for a few minutes.

Feel your body relax; your head is lighter; your neck has no tension. You might even want to stretch your neck from side to side, still breathing slowly.

You can relax your chest with a few deep breaths.

You can relax your belly, feeling the air fill it as you breathe in.

You can relax your hips, your butt, your legs. Feel the tension release from your legs.

You can flex and twist your feet as they relax as well.

Now slowly open your eyes and read the meditation to yourself.

The sky is above; your feet are on Mother Earth.

Each breath and heartbeat reminds you to stay in the "now," moment to moment.

You can see, hear, and touch the world and the presence of others, as well as your own.

You slow down the thought streams.

Breathe slowly to stay "in the now."

You can enjoy the brightness of the sun, the movement of the clouds, or the cold grayness.

You can feel the freshness of the wind, the chill of the darkness of the night, all the splendid and powerful elements of nature that remind you that you are not in control.

You are "alive" and "in the now."

Close your eyes and wander for twenty minutes in meditation, wherever that takes you. When you're done, open your eyes, sit and watch for a few minutes as the world continues to change, moment by moment, heartbeat by heartbeat.

Mindful Step #7:

RECOGNIZE VULNERABLE STATES OF BODY AND MIND

Goal: I will recognize vulnerable body and mind states by using HALTS.

Mantra: HALTS

HALTS is a valuable tool (a mnemonic) to remind you that you are vulnerable to making bad decisions when you are: **H**ungry, **A**ngry, **L**onely, **T**ired, or **S**ick.

Think back to a time when you said something awful to someone you care about or made a decision that had negative consequences. Reflecting back on this situation, you might wonder, "What was I thinking?"

Over the last thirty years of counseling clients, I have often heard clients say, "It seemed like a good idea at the time," when talking about bad decisions they made. Clients also remember invoking the "screw it" attitude. At the time, they essentially said to themselves, "Oh well, I know this is a bad idea, but I am going to do it anyway."

Many of the people making these bad decisions were influenced by being hungry, angry, lonely, tired, or sick (HALTS) at the time that the decisions were being made. For example, many couples have regretted escalated arguments about their marriage when they should have calmed down, had something to eat, and gotten some rest instead of continuing in a "tireless debate."

This mindful step reminds you to recognize when you are hungry, angry, lonely, tired, or sick and to address these vulnerable states of body and mind (see below).

ADDRESSING THE HALTS DYNAMIC

Address the HALTS dynamic by:

Hungry—Feeding the hunger.

Angry—Quieting anger and regaining compassion.

Lonely—Dealing with loneliness and making connection.

Tired—Resting, relaxing, and recreating to renew energy and address fatigue.

Sick—Healing and nurturing yourself out of sickness and back to wellness.

Hungry

Eating in America is often a rushed activity. Eating on the run, eating fast food, and gobbling down something is a too frequent occurrence. How many times have you eaten something and not been consciously aware of what and how much you've eaten? This is a sign of being distracted and not present while eating.

We need to be more aware of when we are hungry and when we are not. We often eat out of habit, boredom, anxiety, and depression.

Christina Feldman, in her book *Beginner's Guide to Buddhist Meditation*, describes mindful eating: "Mindful eating asks that we ensure that we sit down to eat, that it is a moment of calm during our day, and that we remain present as we taste, chew and swallow, one bite at a time." She suggests that you bring a "gentle awareness" to eating: "In much the same way as walking or breathing, the everyday act of eating is transformed when you bring a gentle awareness."

Another important mindful eating practice is to have the conscious awareness of when you are becoming full and to stop eating at that point.

MINDFUL EATING (ME)

Be mindful to:

- Understand the relationship of "mood to food."
- Identify when you are hungry and when you are not hungry.
- Take the time to eat.
- Eat "gently" and slowly, tasting each bite.
- Enjoy meals with others.
- Stop eating when you begin to feel full.

Angry

"If you get angry easily, it may be
because the seed of anger in you has been
watered frequently over many years, and
unfortunately you have allowed it
or even encouraged it to be watered."

—Thich Nhat Hanh, *Taming the Tiger Within*

Anger is a difficult emotion to control because it has some very powerful, even addictive, physiological and psychological reinforcers. The high arousal state of fight or flight is enervating. Your body in the "fight" mode is on alert. All systems are activated—your heart beats faster and stronger, more blood is flowing through your system, your hands may shake, your jaw tightens, and your muscles are tense.

Slowing down anger once it has progressed is difficult. It is better to be aware of anger as it is arising and to address it then. This requires anger awareness and a mindful intervention to a more gentle, understanding, and respectful awareness. If you can become more "aware" of anger, you can challenge yourself to turn it around.

"When a powerfully driven emotion gives way to simple
awareness, it is like a miracle. What emerged
from awareness wasn't screams and accusations
but laughter and insight.
Can we question, while we are angry, whether we
are actually upsetting and intimidating to other people?
Maybe we don't really want to upset other people.
A fresh moment of clarity and insight brings
astonishing sensitivity and care."

—Toni Packer, *The Wonder of Presence*

Rather than having the heavy heart of anger, return to having compassion for yourself and others, being more gentle and patient.

Would You Rather Be Right or Happy?

Instead of respecting each other, people often argue about who is right. They argue about things that don't really matter in the long run. I was counseling a couple recently who spent most of a session arguing about which bananas were cheaper. They were arguing whether the bananas at Costco (factoring in the spoilage factor since there are a lot of bananas in the bundle) or the small bunch of bananas on sale at the local grocery store were cheaper.

When you are in the throws of anger, calm down and take the time to ask yourself if you would rather be right or happy.

ADDRESSING ANGER

Be mindful to:

- Own what you say and do.
- Take responsibility for your actions and decisions.
- Avoid trying to convince others that they are wrong.
- Avoid "tireless debates."
- Develop anger awareness.
- Be "happy" rather than "right."
- Be gentle and patient rather than angry and aggressive.

Lonely

Whatever the cause, loneliness can be a vulnerable state of mind. Mindfulness helps you learn how to deal with loneliness.

"The more we come to terms with
our own separateness, taught the Buddha,
the more we can feel the connections
that are already there."

—Mark Epstein, *Going to Pieces Without Falling Apart*

Cool Loneliness

Pema Chodron, in her book *When Things Fall Apart*, describes cool loneliness:

> Usually we regard loneliness as an enemy. Heartache is not something we choose to invite in. It's restless and pregnant and hot with the desire to escape and find something or someone to keep us company. When we can rest in the middle, we begin to have nonthreatening relationship with loneliness, a relaxing and cooling loneliness that completely turns our usual fearful patterns upside down.

ADDRESSING LONELINESS

Be mindful to:

- Work through feelings of loneliness.
- Develop "cool" loneliness.
- Accept your own separateness.
- Counter loneliness with connection.
- Realize that loneliness will pass with time.

Tired

Being tired can be exhibited in many forms—physical fatigue, emotional exhaustion, feeling stressed out, or just feeling overwhelmed.

Our high-stress, high-energy, competitive American work ethic can result in many people pushing themselves beyond normal capacities and healthy levels of endurance. We pride ourselves in America for working harder, and longer, as a competitive edge over other nations. It is the credo of our immigrant roots. It is the American way to have long workweeks and short vacations. If you combine this with personal, family, and household responsibilities, the result is that the American family is exhausted at the end of the day, sitting and watching television, trying to muster some energy to repeat this pattern again the next day. No wonder people neglect themselves and do not recognize how stressed and fatigued they are.

ADDRESSING TIREDNESS

Be mindful to:

- Evaluate when you might be overdoing it.
- Balance your work and home life.
- Balance work with fun.
- Make time to do things you enjoy.
- Take regular breaks (rest and renewal).
- Don't be so hard on yourself.

Sick

Keep health and wellness as a mindful priority. Being sick reminds us to value and celebrate good health. Whatever life problems come your way, remember to value good health. This might be a simple and obvious observation, but it is one that we often forget to focus on. When we are physically and emotionally well, we often forget to value, celebrate, and have gratitude for our good health.

A good strategy is to value, seek, and do everything possible to be in good health.

ADDRESSING SICKNESS

Be mindful to:

- Make physical and emotional health your top priority.
- Take better care of yourself.
- Value, celebrate, and have gratitude for good health.
- Commit to preventive maintenance and restorative health practices.

Mindful Activities for Recognizing Vulnerable States

Your Mantra Is "HALTS"

HALTS reminds you that you are vulnerable when you are hungry, angry, lonely, tired, or sick. Start your day by repeating your mantra "HALTS" in morning meditation. Repeat "HALTS" to remind yourself to be gentle, understanding, and compassionate to yourself and others when hungry, angry, lonely, tired, or sick.

Reread This Step to Yourself and to Others

As you did with the previous mindful steps, reread this step to yourself. This will keep HALTS as the focus and will remind you to be aware of vulnerable states of body and mind in your daily life. It is also beneficial to read this step out loud to your partner/spouse, your children, or others who are close to you.

Mindful Eating

For one week, keep a diary of your mindful eating. Answer the following questions:

1. Are you consciously aware of when you are full, and do you stop eating at that point?
2. Do you eat with "gentle awareness," slowing down and enjoying each bite, tasting your food?
3. Do you eat when you are not hungry?
4. Do you eat on the rush, grabbing whatever you can?
5. Do you take the time to eat and enjoy a meal with others?

Evaluate how you did and notice any trends. Identify what changes you can make to eat more mindfully.

Meditation

Find a comfortable place to sit. Make yourself comfortable, on a chair or couch with your back straight and your arms resting on your lap, palms up, holding your left hand in your right palm, thumbs slightly touching.

Gently close your eyes and focus on your breath.

Breathe in slowly through your nose and exhale all your breath. Breathe in, filling your abdomen with air. Hold your breath counting to four, then exhale fully. Then breathe slowly and calmly for a few minutes.

Feel your body relax; your head is lighter; your neck has no tension. You might even want to stretch your neck from side to side, still breathing slowly.

You can relax your chest with a few deep breaths.

You can relax your belly, feeling the air fill it as you breathe in.

You can relax your hips, your butt, your legs. Feel the tension release from your legs.

You can flex and twist your feet as they relax as well.

Now slowly open your eyes and read the meditation to yourself.

Slow down. Stop running around. Take a breath.

Breathe slowly. Allow yourself to relax and quiet the thought streams focusing on what you have to do.

Forget about accomplishing. Things will get done in their due time. No but's. They will be there when you get back.

The urgency is self-imposed; that is almost always the case.

Relax, and rest.

Find a comfortable spot to rest your head on a pillow. Let your mind and body continue to relax. Imagine being treated for your fatigue, mood, hunger, and illness in an imaginary facility that can nurse you back to well-being.

Slowly close your eyes and let yourself be comforted and treated; let your imagination create whatever is best for you. After twenty minutes, slowly open your eyes and journal what the experience entailed.

Mindful Step #8:

EMBRACE HEALTHY HABITS —EXERCISE AND FLOW

Goal: I will exercise regularly and seek healthy flow states.

Mantra: FLOW

Exercise

We all know that exercise helps keep the body healthy, but we tend to underestimate how much exercise helps the mind. Of all the healthy habits from flossing to eating right, exercise is probably the most important.

Physical activity is the remedy prescribed most often for mood disorders (such as depression). Exercising three times a week will help improve mood, attitude, health, body, and mind. One of the benefits of exercise is the production of endorphins (natural painkillers), dopamine, and other neurotransmitters. Exercise helps to clear and cleanse the mind and body.

Flow

Mihaly Csikszentmihalyi, author of *Flow: The Psychology of Optimal Experience,* defines flow as: "When consciousness is harmoniously ordered, and you pursue what you are doing for the sheer sake of doing it." The individual is concentrating so completely and is so focused that the depth of observation is optimal and awareness is expanded without tension, making the effort seem effortless. Flow is a state of active attention with relaxation.

Flow can occur with almost any activity. I am an avid tennis player. There are times when I am so aligned and focused during a game that I can get into a flow state. I am in a "zone." I can see the seam on the ball as it is returned. I can anticipate where the ball is going before my opponent has actually struck it. I move to the position on the court where I can best strike and return the ball. The ball seems to come back over the net in slow motion. I can sense my opponent's nervousness as he realizes he is out of position and at risk of losing the point. I focus exclusively on the ball, preparing my backhand return of his cross-court backhand. I am in position, ready and aligned, and waiting to hit the ball on the rise. On contact, I can feel the ball hit the sweet spot on my racket as I shift my weight forward, powering my two-handed backhand into the ball with a low-to-high finish, creating the optimal topspin. I follow through, my racket smoothly finishing over my right shoulder as I watch the ball approach the net. Rotating end over end, the ball clears the net, starts its topspin arc downward, landing low at midcourt. My opponent has no chance to even reach my return. The ball lands three inches—a safe margin—within the sideline. The second bounce lands three feet within the baseline, a perfect backhand winner. I walk away calmly to await the next serve by my opponent, acting as if I play this way all the time, strutting like Andre Agassi.

In *Flow*, Csikszentmihalyi further describes flow as being "so involved in the activity that nothing else seems to matter." As soon as we let outside thoughts or distractions enter into our consciousness, we are likely to come out of the flow state. We would all love to stay in the optimal flow zone. In the previous example, even as I walked away to await the start of the next point, I was aware that the next point might be a different experience. If I don't stay present—"in the now"—or if I am distracted from full concentration, the flow will begin to ebb. Even trained professional athletes will experience ebb and flow in the tides of their ability to focus and concentrate. Sometimes, no matter what we do, we are unable to deflect the distractions, and we will certainly have trouble getting into a "mindful flow." All we can do is evaluate, make the best adjustment to focus, and relax.

Wouldn't it be great if we could always stay in a flow state? However, the very nature of flow involves fluctuations. Any activity, whether gardening, writing a paper, talking with a spouse/partner, developing an existing or new skill, enjoying a walk in nature, work, or tasks like doing the laundry, can result in a flow state (that is, an experience when time seems to pass without consciousness). You may suddenly realize that while you were intently talking with someone much time has gone by. You check your watch and see you have been talking for over an hour, but it seemed like only ten minutes. Sometimes your mind-set and the environment allow you to concentrate easily and get into a flow state. You can often shift without much effort into a flow state, even when stuck in traffic or in other stressful situations.

True Story: Flow and the California Highway Patrolman

A number of years ago while living in Southern California, I had a close encounter with a California highway patrolman (CHP). I had just finished counseling some clients. They all were doing well, showing improvement, and some had breakthroughs that very evening. It was Thursday, and I was looking forward to a long weekend, as this was the end of my workweek.

The sky was clear, with a dusky hue. It was one of those magical evenings that the Mamas & the Papas sang about in "California Dreamin'." I opened my sunroof and rolled down the windows as the fresh night breeze swept through the car. I was thinking about how good life was and how it was good to be alive. I was in a "flow" state, present with my surroundings. Apparently I was not so present though, as I spotted a CHP in my rearview mirror. I glanced down at my speedometer and saw that I was going about ten miles per hour over the speed limit. I knew he was going to pull me over, but I was determined not to get out of the pleasant mood and flow state. I still was focused on how beautiful the night was and how good it was to be alive. A speeding ticket seemed so irrelevant as the full moon was shining brightly on both of us.

As the CHP walked to my car, I was determined to stay in this flow state. We had a routine conversation about my speed, and then something came over me. I looked him squarely in eye and told him about my work with my clients that night and how magical the evening was. Then I said it:

"Officer, I am in a flow state, an altered state of consciousness, mindfully in the now, and it is wonderful!"

He checked my eyes out, wondering if I had been smoking marijuana. When he saw they were clear, he smiled. I smiled back, and we both were quiet, enjoying the silence and cool wonder of the night. He told me to be careful, and I agreed to watch my speed.

He said, "Have a good evening," and walked back to his car without giving me a ticket.

This is a true story. However, I have never tried it again. I don't want to press my luck, but rather I cherish this as a unique experience of "flow."

Mindful Activities for Exercise and Flow

Your Mantra Is "Flow"

Repeat "flow" to remind yourself to concentrate fully, with awareness and relaxation. Start your day by repeating your mantra "flow" in morning meditation.

Reread This Step to Yourself and to Others

As you did with the previous mindful steps, reread this step to yourself. This will keep "flow" as the focus and will remind you to exercise on a regular basis and to engage in positive activities in which you can attain flow in your daily life. It is also beneficial to read this chapter out loud to your partner/spouse, your children, or others who are close to you.

Exploring Flow

1. In your journal, list some forms of exercise that you enjoy and can do regularly.
2. List some new activities or hobbies that are of interest and that you might engage in.
3. Identify those activities that provide:
   - Feelings of mastery
   - Pleasure and enjoyment
   - Release of stress/tension
   - Help with prevention of relapse to unhealthy behaviors
4. Choose an activity that has the three *A*'s—**A**ttractive, **A**ttainable, and **A**ffirming. From all the activities listed above, choose one that you can do to attain flow, and begin or renew doing that activity. Make an action statement about that activity (for example: I am going to play tennis twice a week).

Flow Meditation

Find a comfortable place to sit. Make yourself comfortable, on a chair or couch with your back straight and your arms resting on your lap, palms up, holding your left hand in your right palm, thumbs slightly touching.

Gently close your eyes and focus on your breath.

Breathe in slowly through your nose and exhale all your breath. Breathe in, filling your abdomen with air. Hold your breath counting to four, then exhale fully. Then breathe slowly and calmly for a few minutes.

Feel your body relax; your head is lighter; your neck has no tension. You might even want to stretch your neck from side to side, still breathing slowly.

You can relax your chest with a few deep breaths.

You can relax your belly, feeling the air fill it as you breathe in.

You can relax your hips, your butt, your legs. Feel the tension release from your legs.

You can flex and twist your feet as they relax as well.

Now slowly open your eyes and read the meditation to yourself.

Flow is a state of active attention with relaxation.

You are concentrating so completely and are so focused that the depth of observation is optimal and awareness is expanded without tension, making the effort seem effortless.

Allow your mind to float freely to activities you enjoy doing. This could be making the best egg omelet or climbing a mountain.

Whatever the activity, imagine yourself doing it with flow.

Experience the activities, the interactions, the visceral experiences, in this flow state.

Slowly close your eyes and begin your twenty-minute meditation. After opening your eyes, journal what you experienced. Describe in detail what it was like. Also share your experience and commitment to healthy flow and exercise with someone who will support your commitments and efforts.

Mindful Step #9:
MAKE CONNECTIONS

Goal: I will develop my own support system. I will be involved with others, ask for help and support, and give help and support to others as well.

Mantra: CONNECTION

"To be in good company, you have
to be good company."

—Richard Fields

Connection Starts with Compassion for Self

"You must not withdraw from people when you feel hurt. Instead think actively of ways you can improve your sensitivity to relationships. One's capacity for friendship, which can be developed, is basic to one's capacity for happiness."

—Maxwell Maltz, *Creative Living for Today*

Having compassion for yourself is a precursor to having compassion for others. Bitterness, anger, resentment, shame, and unresolved grief all block the path of making connections with others. It is in the wake of healing that compassion and connection can be made with others.

Asking for Help and Support from Others

"There are times when we may honestly say 'I am suffering; please help.' Just as there are times when it is appropriate to say 'I see that you are suffering; I am here.'"

—David Brazier, *The Feeling Buddha*

We all need support. The people who support and encourage you are your "support group" or support system. The key element of a support group is a common interest, goal, mission, or task.

You Can't Do It Alone: Finding and Working with a Teacher/Counselor

"Some teachers are rascals and coyotes
who trick and surprise their students;
Some are harsh taskmasters trying to
whittle down ego and pride;
Others teach more through honoring
and encouragement, nurturing the best in a student;
Some teachers lecture like a professor;
Others can melt us open
with their love and compassion.
The greatest and simplest power of
a teacher is the environment
of their own freedom and joy."

—Jack Kornfield, *A Path with Heart*

Having a teacher, a mentor, a coach, a counselor, or a confidant is an essential lifeline, especially when parents either do not have these skills or are not available. This true story illustrates the importance of a connection with such a mentor.

True Story: Patrick and the Librarian

Patrick Carnes, Ph.D., is well known in the addictions field. He has specialized in sex addiction, has presented regularly throughout the United States and internationally, and has written several groundbreaking books on the topic of sex addiction. He has trained thousands of therapists to become certified in sex addiction and has worked with many treatment centers. He is clearly the most accomplished person in the sex addictions field.

Patrick was a victim of abuse as a child, and he tells this story to highlight the importance of having a person who acts as a mentor, coach, even mother figure, especially when your family is fragmented by abuse.

As a young child, Patrick always had a passion for reading. It was a way to escape unpleasant feelings and enter other worlds. The librarian in his hometown noticed this and helped Patrick to develop this passion. She would talk with Patrick about what he liked to read. She would then save books for him and sit and talk with him about the books. She frequently turned him on to new areas of interest, expanding his awareness.

They would sit and talk about books, life, current events, and the things that were happening in Patrick's life. She became his teacher/mentor, and a relationship developed that gave Patrick consistency and safety. She was someone he could trust and count on. This relationship went on for several years until Patrick moved and lost contact with the librarian.

It was more than thirty years later, and Patrick, now an accomplished professional, was telling this story to a training group to illustrate how important one person can be in a child's life. A man in the audience said, "Dr. Carnes, I know the woman you are talking about." There was a pregnant pause, as Patrick and the audience of counselors were surprised by this man's assertion. They all looked at him wondering what he would say next. The man slowly stood up, pushing his seat back, and said, "Yes, that woman who helped you is my wife, and she is here today, sitting right next to me."

You could imagine the tears of joy and the heartfelt connection as Patrick went and hugged this woman. Tears rolled down both their faces, as well as the faces of most of the people in attendance.

CONNECTIONS

You make connections with others by:

- Developing compassion for yourself and others.
- Developing your own support group.
- Seeking the help of a teacher.
- Asking for help and support when you need it.
- Helping and supporting others.

Mindful Activities for Making Connections

Your Mantra Is "Connection"

Repeat "connection" to remind yourself to be involved with others, while letting others be involved with you. Start your day by repeating your mantra "connection" in morning meditation.

Reread This Step to Yourself and to Others

As you did with the previous mindful steps, reread this step to yourself. This will keep "connection" as the focus and will remind you to maintain connection and compassion with others in your daily life. It is also of benefit to read this step out loud to your partner/spouse, your children, or others who are close to you.

Connection on the Occasion of Your Birthday

On the occasion of your next birthday, call all those people in your support system before they have a chance to call you. Thank them for their support, sacrifice, and encouragement. Tell them you care about (and love) them, and give a specific example of their support. Notice their reaction and affirm the importance of the relationship.

Connection Meditation

Find a comfortable place to sit. Make yourself comfortable, on a chair or couch with your back straight and your arms resting on your lap, palms up, holding your left hand in your right palm, thumbs slightly touching.

Gently close your eyes and focus on your breath.

Breathe in slowly through your nose and exhale all your breath. Breathe in, filling your abdomen with air. Hold your breath counting to four, then exhale fully. Then breathe slowly and calmly for a few minutes.

Feel your body relax; your head is lighter; your neck has no tension. You might even want to stretch your neck from side to side, still breathing slowly.

You can relax your chest with a few deep breaths.

You can relax your belly, feeling the air fill it as you breathe in.

You can relax your hips, your butt, your legs. Feel the tension release from your legs.

You can flex and twist your feet as they relax as well.

Now slowly open your eyes and read the meditation to yourself.

You are going on a "journey of connection."

You are to choose people to bring with you, people who are part of your support system. You can bring friends, family, colleagues, children, adults, even pets, and so on. You are also encouraged to bring teachers, mentors, and other people you admire.

You might want to choose some new people or people you don't know well but want to get to know.

Do not worry if they are available or not—this is your fantasy journey.

Make a mental list of all of those people you want to take with you. You can make it a few people or many; it is up to you.

Then think about the places you want to go, the means of travel, and what you might want to do. Just think about this in a general sense, unless there is something special you want to do or someplace special you want to go.

Relax, breathe slowly, and begin your journey. Close your eyes, *let your heart be your compass*, and spend the next twenty minutes on your "journey of connection." Remember to journal after you are done. Journal about your journey. You might want to answer these questions in your journal:

Who did you bring with you?
What significant connections occurred?
Who did you feel most connected to? Why?
Who were the most important sources of support? How?
Were there any surprises?

Mindful Step #10:
FOCUS ON THE TEN ELEMENTS OF SUCCESS

Goal: I will identify and apply the ten elements of success.

Mantra: SUCCESS

Strength of Mind

A strong mind will see with clarity what was once blurred by anxiety, depression, anger, and fear. By practicing the first nine mindful steps, you will have a stronger mind. A strong mind can overcome limitations and achieve beyond what was once imagined. We exercise our bodies; we also need to exercise our minds. A strong mind can deal with adversity and have courage and compassion.

Defining Success

Success is defined in many different ways. Success is something we all seek in our lives. However, each of us has our own definition of success based on our many roles. For parents, success is raising their children effectively and having the ability to provide for the family. For workers, success is a sense of professional accomplishment. For entrepreneurs, success is the creation of something new or better. For artists, success is a piece of work that is an expression of their soul. For couples/partners, success is a connected, fulfilling relationship. For politicians, success is improving the community and the system. For philanthropists, success is the contribution to improving the quality of others' lives and making the world a better place.

Sometimes our definitions of success are replaced with goals that may not be so altruistic. Over time we may lose our original visions, resulting in misplaced values. For example:

- The mother who lives through her children's accomplishments, not her own
- The father who fails to be present for his family, putting work before them
- The worker who stops caring about his/her work and is no longer interested in the outcome and is just going through the motions
- The entrepreneur who defines success as winning at all

costs for his or her own gain, regardless of the impact on others

- The artist who abandons creativity for the visions of others
- The couple/partners who stop working on the relationship
- The politician who defines success as reelection, despite the needs of his or her constituents
- The philanthropist who loses sight of his or her contribution and lets ego get in the way

These examples remind us to constantly review and perhaps revise our definitions of success. These false senses of success can give us the illusion that we are "successful," but not the feeling that we have virtue and integrity.

Ten Key Elements of Success

You can strengthen your own success by understanding and viewing these elements of success with more clarity and focus. The ten key mindful elements of success are:

1. Talents and skills with virtue
2. Intuition
3. Passion and motivation

4. Maintaining optimism and tolerating rejection
5. The desire to learn, discover, and grow
6. Freedom of choice—staying "in the now"
7. Creativity—ability to be flexible and to change
8. Connection and a strong support system
9. Timing and luck
10. Not taking life so seriously

1. Talents and Skills with Virtue

Everyone has unique talents and skills. Mindfulness involves learning to use your talents and skills with compassion and virtue, while sheltering the fire of the ego.

"Fame is not gained through talent alone.
It is better to have virtue without talent
than talent without virtue. Thus it is impossible
to lead a Chan community without talent,
but it is also impossible for someone
who relies exclusively on talent. Therefore
in nominating talented people
(to leadership positions) in a Chan community,
account must be taken of their virtue."

—Chan Master Sheng Yen, *Attaining the Way*

2. Intuition

"When something bites you in the butt, go for it!"

—Irvin Yalom, M.D.

I have had the good fortune to have Dr. Irvin Yalom as a presenter at a few of my conferences. The multitalented Dr. Yalom, besides having written two college textbooks, has also written several novels, my favorite being *When Nietzsche Wept*. In talking with Irv, he once told me that when something "bites you in the butt, go for it." His books have been written with this discovery of being "bitten in the butt."

Whatever the endeavor, when something gets your positive attention, or "bites you in the butt," it is an indication that you need to pay attention to it. I would suggest that those things that get your positive attention are often the things that are built on your talents and skills.

3. Passion and Motivation

"Aspiration is a glowing flame that secretly and sacredly uplifts our consciousness and finally liberates us."

—Sri Chinmoy, *The Wisdom of Sri Chinmoy*

In order to be successful, you need to harness your passion and motivation. Accept periods of low passion and motivation, and work through the issues that are blocking your heart. Recognize there are periods like this and that this can and will change.

4. Maintaining Optimism and Tolerating Rejection

People's belief that they are going to be successful is a highly correlated factor with success. In the counseling field, the factor most highly correlated with success with clients is the counselors' belief that they will be able to help their clients.

Maintaining a positive, realistic optimism is essential for success. The ability to put rejections and setbacks into a realistic perspective promotes optimism. The reactive elements of pessimism (seeing things as permanent, pervasive, and personal) can undermine success.

5. The Desire to Learn, Discover, and Grow

"Learning is nothing but discovery
that something is possible. To teach means
to show a person that something is possible."

—Frederick S. Perls, *Gestalt Therapy Verbatim*

Success involves the desire to explore what is out there and what is possible.

6. Freedom of Choice—Staying "in the Now"

You always have choices. You may be in a situation where your choices are limited "in the now," but you still have the freedom to make choices. Opportunities will arise in time. Sometimes the best thing you can do is stay "in the now" and make the best choice at each opportunity, one decision at a time, one day at a time.

7. Creativity—Ability to Be Flexible and to Change

Creative intelligence can be defined as thinking of new applications of your talents and skills. The "creative self" is a powerful and integral part of success because it involves the ability to be flexible and to change.

8. Connection and a Strong Support System

Being aware of the importance of a strong support system and connections is the force that powers continued success.

9. Timing and Luck

"May the force be with you."

—*Star Wars*

Being aware of how you can put yourself in a position to have the right timing and luck is a key element to being successful. Being in the right place, at the right time, in the right mindful frame is another integral element in success. Timing and luck also involve having the patience and perseverance to continue to put yourself in situations that lead to success.

10. Not Taking Life So Seriously

Try to maintain a good sense of humor. Learn to laugh at the mysteries of life. Learn to laugh at yourself and to not take yourself so seriously. See the humorous side of our human existence.

"Don't aim at success—the more you aim at it and make
it a target, the more you are going to miss it.
For success, like happiness, cannot be pursued;
it must ensue, and it only does so as the unintended
side-effect of one's personal dedication to a cause

greater than oneself or as the product of one's surrender to a person other than oneself. Happiness must happen, and the same holds for success: you have to let it happen by not caring about it."

—Viktor Frankl, *Man's Search for Meaning*

Mindful Activities for Success

Your Mantra Is "Success"

Gently repeat "success" to remind yourself to keep the ten elements of success in your consciousness. When experiencing either setbacks or rejections, repeat the mantra "success" to refocus on what you can do to persevere "in the now." Start your day by repeating your mantra "success" in morning meditation.

Reread This Step to Yourself and to Others

As you did with the previous mindful steps, reread this step to yourself. This will keep "success" as the focus and will remind you to maintain and invoke the ten elements of success in your daily life. It is also of benefit to read this step out loud to your partner/spouse, your children, or others who are close to you.

Prioritize the 10 Elements of Success

1. Rank the ten elements of success in order of importance. Rank what you think is the most important element first (1) and the least important last (10).

_____ Talents and skills with virtue

_____ Intuition

_____ Passion and motivation

_____ Maintaining optimism and tolerating rejection

_____ Desire to learn, discover, and grow

_____ Freedom of choice

_____ Creativity—ability to be flexible and to change

_____ Connection and a strong support system

_____ Timing and luck

_____ Not taking life so seriously

2. Now rank the same list in terms of your own skills. Rank the skill you have the most first (1) and the skill you have the least last (10).

_____ Talents and skills with virtue

_____ Intuition

_____ Passion and motivation

_____ Maintaining optimism and tolerating rejection

_____ Desire to learn, discover, and grow

_____ Freedom of choice

_____ Creativity—ability to be flexible and to change

_____ Connection and a strong support system

_____ Timing and luck

_____ Not taking life so seriously

3. For each element, subtract its importance ranking from the ranking for your own skill. This will help you identify the skills you are most deficient in and need to work on. For example, if you ranked passion and motivation as the most important skill (1), and you ranked it number 10 in your personal ranking, then 10 – 1 = +9, a very high score that indicates you need to work on passion and motivation.

4. What are the top four elements of success that you need to work on based on this scale and their relative scores?

Success Meditation

Find a comfortable place to sit. Make yourself comfortable, on a chair or couch with your back straight and your arms resting on your lap, palms up, holding your left hand in your right palm, thumbs slightly touching.

Gently close your eyes and focus on your breath.

Breathe in slowly through your nose and exhale all your breath. Breathe in, filling your abdomen with air. Hold your breath counting to four, then exhale fully. Then breathe slowly and calmly for a few minutes.

Feel your body relax; your head is lighter; your neck has no tension. You might even want to stretch your neck from side to side, still breathing slowly.

You can relax your chest with a few deep breaths.

You can relax your belly, feeling the air fill it as you breathe in.

You can relax your hips, your butt, your legs. Feel the tension release from your legs.

You can flex and twist your feet as they relax as well.

Now slowly open your eyes and read the meditation to yourself.

Think of all the joy and success you have had in your life. The triumphs over periodic challenges and the appreciation of each day.

Meditate for the next twenty minutes, focusing on your gratitude for all your joy and success. Upon opening your eyes, journal about your meditation, writing your observations and experience of your joy and success.

There you are!

REFERENCES

Beck, Aaron, *Depression,* University of PA Press, 1972.

Birx, Ellen. *Healing Zen: Awakening to Life of Wholeness and Compassion While Caring for Yourself and Others.* New York: Viking, 2002.

Bowen, Sarah, Heharika Chawla, G. Alan Marlatt, George A. Parks. MBRP Mindfulness-Based Relapse Prevention, Facilitation Summary, April 2007.

Bowen, Sarah, Katie Witkiewitz, Tiara M. Dillworth, G. Alan Marlatt (2007). "The role of thought suppression in the relationship between mindfulness, meditation, and alcohol use." *Addictive Behaviors* 32, 2323–2328.

Brach, Tara. *Radical Acceptance: Embracing Your Life with the Heart of a Buddha.* New York: Bantam, 2004.

Brazier, David. *The Feeling Buddha: A Buddhist Psychology of Character, Adversity, and Passion.* New York: Fromm International, 1997.

Chinmoy, Sri. *The Wisdom of Sri Chinmoy,* First Edition. San Diego, CA: Blue Dove Press, 2000.

Chodron, Pema. *Comfortable with Uncertainty: 108 Teachings on Cultivating Fearlessness and Compassion.* Boston: Shambhala, 2002.

Chodron, Pema. *The Places that Scare You: A Guide to Fearlessness in Different Times.* Boston: Shambhala, 2001.

Chodron, Pema. *Start Where You Are: A Guide to Compassionate Living.* Boston: Shambhala, 2001.

Chodron, Pema. *When Things Fall Apart: Heart Advice for Difficult Times.* Boston: Shambhala, 2000.

Chodron, Thubten. *Open Heart, Clear Mind.* Ithaca, NY: Snow Lion Publications, 1990.

Csikszentmihalyi, Mihaly. *Flow: The Psychology of Optimal Experience.* New York: Harper Perennial, 1991.

Epstein, Mark. *Going to Pieces Without Falling Apart: Lessons from Meditation and Psychotherapy.* New York: Broadway Books, 1998.

Feldman, Christina. *Beginner's Guide to Buddhist Meditation: Practices for Mindful Living.* Berkeley, CA: Rodmell Press, 2006

Fields, Richard. *Drugs in Perspective,* 6th edition. New York: McGraw-Hill, 2006.

Fossum, Merle, and Marilyn Mason. *Facing Shame: Families in Recovery.* New York: Norton, 1989.

Frankl, Viktor. *Man's Search for Meaning,* New York: Simon & Schuster, 1959.

Gottman, John. *Why Marriages Succeed or Fail: And How You Can Make Yours Last.* New York: Simon & Schuster, 1995.

Goldstein, Joseph. *One Dharma: The Emerging Western Buddhism.* New York: HarperOne, 2002.

Hagen, Steve. *Buddhism Plain and Simple.* New York: Broadway Books, 1997.

Hayes, Steven, Victoria Follette, and Marsha Linehan, (Eds.). *Mindfulness and Acceptance: Expanding the Cognitive-Behavioral Tradition.* New York: Guilford Press, 2004.

Hayes, S.C., Strosahl, K.D., and Wilson, K.G. *Acceptance and Commitment Therapy: An Experiential Approach to Behavior Change.* New York: Guilford Press, 1998.

Kabat-Zinn, John, "Mindfulness-based interventions in context: Past, present and future," *Clinical Psychology: Science and Practice,* p. 145–146, 2003.

Kabat-Zinn, J., Massion, A., Kristeller, J., Pererson, L.G., Fletcher, K.E., Pbert, L., Lenderking, W.R., and Santorelli, S.F. "Effectiveness of mediation-based stress reduction intervention in the treatment of anxiety disorder," *American Journal of Psychiatry,* 149, 936–943, 1992.

Kaufman, Edward. "The psychotherapy of dually diagnosed patients," *Journal of Substance Abuse Treatment*, 6(1) 9–18, 1989.

Kornfield, Jack. "Beyond Mental Health: Jack Kornfield on Buddhist Psychology for the West." *Inquiring Mind* 14 (Fall 2007): 4–7.

Kornfield, Jack. *A Path with Heart: A Guide Through the Perils and Promises of Spiritual Life*. New York: Bantam, 1993.

Kornfield, Jack. *The Wise Heart: A Guide to the Universal Teachings of Buddhist Psychology*. New York: Bantam, 2008.

Kubler-Ross, Elisabeth. *On Death and Dying*. New York: Scribner, 1997.

Langer, Ellen J. *Mindfulness*. Reading, MA: Addison-Wesley, 1989.

Langer, Ellen, and Judith Rodin. "The Effects of Enhanced Personal Responsibility for the Aged: A Field Experiment in an Institutional Setting." *Journal of Personality and Social Psychology* 34 (1976): 191–198.

Lau, Mark A., and Zindel V. Segal. "Mindfulness-Based Cognitive Therapy as a Relapse Prevention Approach to Depression," in K. A. Witkiewitz and G. A. Marlatt (Eds.), *Therapist's Guide to Evidence-Based Relapse Prevention*. Burlington, MA: Academic Press, 2007.

Linehan, Marsha. *Cognitive-behavioral treatment of borderline personality disorder.* New York: Guildford, 1993.

Maltz, Maxwell. *Creative Living for Today*. New York: Trident Press, , 1967.

Marlatt, Alan. "Buddhist Psychology and the Treatment of Addictive Behavior." *Journal of Cognitive and Behavioral Practice* 9(1) (2002): 44–49.

Marlatt, G. Alan, and Neharika Chawla. "Meditation and Alcohol Use," *Southern Medical Journal,* vol. 100, no. 4, April 2007.

Miller, William, and Janet C'de Baca. *Quantum Change: When Epiphanies and Sudden Insights Transform Ordinary Lives.* New York: Guilford, 2001.

Miller, William, and Stephen Rollnick. *Motivational Interviewing: Preparing People to Change Addictive Behavior.* New York: Guilford, 1992.

Mipham, Sakyong. *Turning the Mind Into an Ally*. New York: Riverhead Books (Penguin Putnam), 2003.

Nhat Hanh, Thich. *Taming the Tiger Within: Meditations on Transforming Difficult Emotions.* New York: Riverhead Books, 2004.

Packer, Toni. *The Wonder of Presence: And the Way of Meditative Inquiry.* Boston: Shambhala, 2002.

Padesky, Christine, and Dennis Greenberger. *Mind Over Mood: Change How You Feel by Changing the Way You Think*. New York: Guilford Press, 1995.

Perls, Frederick S. *Gestalt Therapy Verbatim*. Boulder, CO: Real People Press, 1969.

Rinpoche, Patrul. *The Words of My Perfect Teacher*. NY: Harper-Collins, 1994.

Rothberg, Donald. *The Engaged Spiritual Life: A Buddhist Approach to Transforming Ourselves and the World.* Boston: Beacon Press, 2006.

Sapadin, Linda, and Jack Maguire. *It's About Time! The Six Styles of Procrastination and How to Overcome Them.*New York: Penguin, 1997.

Salzberg, Sharon. *Lovingkindness: The Revolutionary Art of Happiness*. Boston: Shambhala, 1990.

Seligman, Martin. *Learned Optimism: How to Change Your Mind and Your Life.* New York: Knopf, 1990.

Segal, Z., et al. *Mindfulness-Based Cognitive Therapy for Depression: A New Approach to Preventing Relapse.* NY: Guildford Press, 2002.

Tolle, Eckhart. *The Power of Now*. Novato, CA: New World Library, 1999.

Witkiewitz, Katie, G. Alan Marlatt, and Denise Walker. "Mindfulness-based relapse prevention for alcohol and substance use disorders: The meditative tortoise wins the race," Addictive Behavior Research Center, University of Washington, 2007.

Wolin, Steven J., and Sybil Wolin. *The Resilient Self: How Survivors of Troubled Families Rise Above Adversity.* New York: Villard Books, 1993.

Yen, Sheng. *Attaining the Way: A Guide to the Practice of Chan Buddhism.* Boston: Shambhala, 2006.

INDEX

C

D

ABOUT THE AUTHOR

Dr. Richard Fields is a noted author, master teacher, national speaker, seasoned counselor, and expert in the alcohol/drug recovery and treatment field. He has more than thirty-five years of experience in the mental health and alcohol/drug recovery fields. This is demonstrated in his ability to pragmatically explain the application of "mindfulness" in developing healthy and positive change.

Further, Dr. Fields is the author of *Drugs in Perspective*, 6th Edition, McGraw Hill, 2006, a college textbook used in several college and university alcohol/drug studies programs. He is the founder and director of FACES (Family & Addiction Conferences and Educational Seminars, www.facesconferences.com). For more than fifteen years, FACES has been and continues to provide state-of-the-art continuing education conferences to thousands of psychologists, social workers, and mental health and alcohol/drug counselors.

Dr. Fields is a registered counselor in Bellevue, Washington, specializing in a private practice that focuses on alcohol/drug treatment, and is the co-owner of www.mysoberlife.com, an online social support network for alcohol/drug recovery and relapse prevention.